IF YOU
LIKE
THE
BEATLES...

Also by Bruce Pollock

In Their Own Words: Lyrics and Lyricists
The Face of Rock & Roll: Images of a Generation
Playing for a Change
Me, Minsky, & Max
It's Onlly Rock and Roll
The Disco Handbook
When Rock was Young
When the Music Mattered: Rock in the 1960s
Hipper Than Our Kids: A Rock & Roll Journal of the Baby Boom Generation
Rock Song Index: The 7500 Most Important Songs of the Rock Era, 1944-2000
Working Musicians: Defining Moments from the Road, the Studio, and the Stage(E-book)
By the Time We Got to Woodstock: The Great Rokck 'n' Roll Revolution of 1969
When the Music Mattered: Portraits from the 1960s (e-book reissue)
It's Only Rock and Roll (E-boook reissue)

IF YOU
LIKE
THE
BEATLES...

HERE ARE **OVER 200** BANDS, FILMS, RECORDS AND OTHER ODDITIES THAT YOU WILL LOVE.

BRUCE POLLOCK

Backbeat Books

AN IMPRINT OF HAL LEONARD CORPORATION

Published in 2011 by Backbeat Books
An Imprint of Hal Leonard Corporation
7777 West Bluemound Road
Milwaukee, WI 53213

Trade Book Division Editorial Offices
33 Plymouth St., Montclair, NJ 07042

Photos courtesy of Photofest

Book design by Michael Kellner

Printed in the United States of America

Library of Congress Cataloging-in-Publication Data
Pollock, Bruce.
  If you like the Beatles : here are over 200 bands, films, records and other oddities that you will love / Bruce Pollock.
     p. cm.
  Includes index.
  ISBN 978-1-61713-018-2 (pbk.)
  1. Beatles. 2. Rock musicians–England. 3. Rock music–History and criticism. I. Title.
  ML421.B4P65 2011
  782.42166092'2--dc23
                                    2011028882
ISBN 978-1-61713-018-2

www.backbeatbooks.com

CONTENTS

IF YOU LIKE
THE BEATLES...

The Beatles, 1964. (© CBS.)

Introduction

BEFORE THERE WERE THE BEATLES

An untold number of hardy souls were prompted to work on their vocal chops and dance moves after seeing Elvis Presley's hip-swiveling debut on *The Ed Sullivan Show* on September 9, 1956.

Buddy Holly's Ed Sullivan stint in December 1957, however, failed to produce any sort of onslaught of jangly guitar bands with a sensitive songwriter at the helm to challenge the prevailing dominance of the Presley rock 'n' roll model: charismatic lead singer flanked by faceless backup players.

But within a few months of the Beatles' three consecutive appearances on *The Ed Sullivan Show*, on February 9, 16, and 23, 1964, ninety percent of the aspiring musicians in America were buying matching suits, ties, and instruments and growing their hair long.

By 1960, the fevered run of wildcat rockabilly and salacious R&B singles that defined the 1950s had given way to malleable girl groups, post-doo-wop Italian crooners, and identical R&B acts with identical time steps. For all-American white collegiate types anxious to be sophisticated, the fraternity house harmonies of folk music gently tweaked the system, from the Kingston Trio and the Brothers Four to the Highwaymen and the Chad Mitchell Trio.

In Philadelphia, Dick Clark was grooming the first graduating class of teen idols—Fabian, Dion, Paul Anka, Bobby Rydell, Freddy Cannon, Neil Sedaka, Frankie Avalon, Brenda Lee, Connie Francis—for lounge careers in Las Vegas or at the Copacabana. In Detroit, Berry Gordy was looking to make black music respectable by emulating the song factories of New York, Los Angeles, and

Nashville, which clung to their franchises in the sometimes thrilling, sometimes tired Tin Pan Alley tradition.

Buddy Holly died in a plane crash in February 1959; Eddie Cochran, in a car crash in April 1960. In 1961 Gene Vincent, Jerry Lee Lewis, Chuck Berry, Little Richard, and the Everly Brothers were either already in or heading toward creative limbo; Elvis was busy making movies; even Wanda Jackson had cleaned up her act. Bob Dylan blew in from Minnesota, a secret rock 'n' roll fan in the guise of a weathered beatnik poet. But Dylan was an acquired taste for a small downscale market.

With no one else to be enamored of, the spreading rock 'n' roll audience became, during the 1960–63 period, enamored of itself. In the image of its new president and his New Frontier, this crowd was old enough to reinvent its antiquated inner Elvis in a new kind of downtown nightlife gyration called the twist. For two years this dull thud dominated the radio dial and the aspirations of local bands.

Through 1963 the idea of a rock band not tied to the mindless rhythm of the twist or the equally mindless (albeit seductive) rhythm of surf music seemed to exist only in Portland, Oregon, where the instrumental group the Wailers, of "Tall Cool One" fame, still occupied a legendary place in the area's rock pantheon.

Paul Revere and the Raiders sent the instrumental track "Like Long Hair," to the Top 40 in 1961, but Revere got drafted and the momentum faded. By 1963 he was back, vying with another local band, the Kingsmen, for the next crack at a 1956 Richard Berry favorite called "Louie Louie" that was kicking up dust on the circuit. Revere got the regional hit, the Kingsmen's version went national. But both paid a price. Signed by Columbia Records' Mitch Miller, who was noted for his antipathy towards rock 'n' roll, Revere and the Raiders were aced by the Kingsmen when Miller failed to promote the Raiders' single.

The Kingsmen may have won the battle, but they lost the war when lead singer Jack Ely quit after "Louie Louie" became a hit to form a new band. The Kingsmen's bass player, who owned the group name, drew the wrath of fans when he lip-synched to Ely's voice at gigs. Paul Revere and the Raiders wouldn't reach the Top 40 again until the end of 1965. No wonder no other major American label wanted to sign anything that smelled like a real rock band.

The most successful new American bands of the 1962–64 period, the Four Seasons (Vee-Jay) and the Beach Boys (Capitol), were essentially throwbacks to earlier, softer eras. The Four Seasons were already warhorses; post-doo-wop Italian soul veterans, with Frankie Valli in the Frankie Lymon falsetto role. The Beach Boys were the Four Freshmen on surfboards, with Brian Wilson still in the creative closet, under the thumb of his father.

President Kennedy was more popular than any rock star. Comedians like Lenny Bruce, Mort Sahl, and Shelley Berman were more relevant. Dylan was in Greenwich Village now, starting to tap into the outcast rage rock 'n' roll had once channeled. Dylan walked off *The Ed Sullivan Show* when Sullivan wouldn't let him sing a song about the John Birch Society. You wouldn't find Dylan on *Hootenanny*, the folk music TV show that blacklisted Pete Seeger. On the other hand, Joey Dee and the Starliters played for the president's wife, showing just how entrenched in the establishment this harmless rock 'n' roll had become.

England wasn't on the typical rock fan's radar then, but a few discerning folks were in on the secret. England was where old rock 'n' roll still mattered. Gene Vincent settled there. Eddie Cochran died there. Buddy Holly had a string of posthumous hits there. In 1964 Paul Simon spent his first divorce from Art Garfunkel busking there. In 1966 the Everly Brothers recorded an album called *Two Yanks in England* there. Amid folk, blues, and classic rock 'n' roll, the Beatles soldiered on, relentlessly playing seven shows a night, the most eclectic bar band in the world. They could segué from era to era as easily as they went from genre to genre. In the meantime, their original songs were starting to get some notice. Once "Please Please Me" hit Number One on the UK singles chart in February 1963, they would notch eleven more in a row (not counting the *Twist and Shout* EP).

The Beatles. Not John Lennon and the Beatles nor Paul McCartney and the Beatles, as rock 'n' roll history would have put it

(John and Paul were both too competitive, especially with each other, to ever let that happen.). Instead, they were a self-contained rock 'n' roll band with three singers and two (sometimes three) great songwriters; even better than the Crickets. But despite the mania the Beatles inspired in England, American music honchos hedged their bets; the first Beatles singles of 1964 in the U.S. were on five different labels.

Before any of these groups inspired by the Beatles on *The Ed Sullivan Show* could find their way to a recording studio, bands from England schooled on American rock 'n' roll were all over the map. Even Bob Dylan took notice, especially that week in April 1964 when the Beatles had all five of the Top Five records. Or that day in September when the Animals took Dylan's arrangement (really Dave Van Ronk's) of "The House of the Rising Sun" to Number One. Later, when the Rolling Stones appeared, half of those aspiring musicians traded in their suits, ties, and smiles for grungy T-shirts and jeans, thus creating the image of the sullen rock band that's been in place ever since, from the Stooges to Nirvana to the White Stripes, at the same time casting the Beatles as hopelessly clean-cut sellouts to American capitalism. But the Beatles had lived the Stones' image for years. Before Brian Epstein spiffed them up for mass consumption they were as sullen as the Replacements.

And Mick Jagger was an economics major.

When the Beatles retired from live performing after about sixty American concert dates, they also suffered in comparison with the Stones—who have since been on the road for forty years—especially when you consider that those sixty concerts were marginal affairs, limited by the logistical nightmares their fame had created. On the other hand, if the live experience of seeing the Beatles ceased to exist after their journeyman stint in Hamburg, those first three *Ed Sullivan Show* appearances were enough to establish a rock band template long missing from American shores. They were enough to hoist the various Beatle singles moldering in radio's slush pile into the Top Five. And they were enough to open the ports at Ellis Island to the whole of singing England.

From there on, with uncanny regularity, whenever a lull in the forward thrust of jangly guitar-based rock 'n' roll set upon the music industry, a Beatlesque solution would emerge to right the ship. Considering the wealth of music that informed the Beatles pre-fame set list, the extraordinary afterlife of the approximately 200 recorded originals they produced and the wealth of music they inspired with their songs, and with their attitude, there is a super-rich catalog of material to hum and sing and contemplate in these pages . . . if you like the Beatles.

Billy Fury, 1960.

1

CROSSING OVER

Landlocked to the conservative programming choices of the BBC in the late 1950s and early 1960s, the Beatles and other British musicians were sustained in their formative years by pirate radio and the import market to provide them with their nightly rush of American singles and roots music. By 1962 the Beatles, partial to stateside rock 'n' roll and the early stalwarts of R&B, became one of the most successful and sought-after cover bands on the continent, prized as much for their versatility as their energy, as apt to toss in a show tune or a traditional evergreen as to showcase the latest Brill Building gem.

Their status was established even before they were introduced to the musical and sartorial preferences of their future manager, record store owner and budding rock journalist Brian Epstein, who saw "the future of rock and roll" one afternoon in 1961 (predating Jon Landau's sighting of Bruce Springsteen by a good dozen years), when he heard the Beatles at Liverpool's Cavern Club. Theirs was a repertoire that certainly impressed their eventual producer George Martin, whose limitless good taste ran from show music and skiffle to the cinematic scores of Johnny Dankworth and the wacked-out comedy of Peter Sellers and Spike Milligan (*The Goon Show*), and Peter Cook and Dudley Moore (*Beyond the Fringe*).

Other considerations aside, perhaps the most significant early influence on the Beatles, individually, collectively, or at least subconsciously, was the major crush they seemed to have, like almost every other British schoolboy of the time, on Rita Tushingham. Tushingham was a young actress who played Jo in the 1961 movie version of *A Taste of Honey*, an adaptation of a play written in 1958 by Shelagh Delaney and set in Saltford, a mere forty-five minutes from Liverpool. Prematurely frumpy, Tushingham was the poor man's Mandy Rice-Davies; the anti-Jean Shrimpton, whose career arguably peaked with her performance as the ugly duckling seventeen-year-old shop girl in the poignant and profound film adaptation.

As popular as they had become on their side of the pond, the Beatles, in their heart of hearts, were still products of the same dead-end streets and thwarted desires as the characters in the play and subsequent movie version of *A Taste of Honey*, looking for a way out. (John's father had been a sailor who, more or less, never returned.) You could see it in their choices of mates, many of whom eerily reflected the sad-eyed Jo. There was the drab sixteen-year-old hairdresser/groupie Maureen Cox, who Ringo started dating in 1962 when he was twenty-two. He would marry her three years later. In that same year of 1962, John married the marginally better-looking and more educated Cynthia Powell after getting her pregnant. He had met her in art school in 1957 when he was seventeen and she, eighteen. In 1964 the twenty-year-old George fell for the slightly buck-toothed shampoo girl and aspiring nineteen-year-old model Pattie Boyd. They married early in 1966. Only Paul had his eyes on a glamorous prize signally beyond his middle class reach, the seventeen-year-old doctor's daughter Jane Asher, who he met in 1963 when he was twenty-one. She would introduce him to high society and high culture, playing the part of artist muse (as Suze Rotolo would for Bob Dylan). Although they became engaged in 1967, they never married.

Paul's sentimental and nostalgic streak would have made him a sucker for *A Taste of Honey* and its evocative occasional theme, which was written by Bobby Scott for the 1960 Broadway production of the play starring Joan Plowright as Jo and Billy Dee Williams as her departed lover. While music was an essential emotional element in the play (characters literally danced onto the stage), provided by the Apex Jazz Trio (Johnny Walback, cornet; Barry Wright, guitar; and Christopher Capon, double bass), the Scott tune eventually became more famous than the show, especially after the movie version won the composer a Grammy for best instrumental recording.

Although Martin Denny's recording of "A Taste of Honey" was the original version, Herb Alpert, a consultant on the film, had the biggest recording of it a few years later. There were also significant covers floating around England by British musicians, including pianist Victor Feldman and clarinetist Acker Bilk. After some appropriately bittersweet lyrics were added by sometime-actor Ric Marlow, a host of vocal versions commenced. One of the first was by the Beatles, who performed it live on the BBC in October 1962 and included it on their first EP, with Paul singing lead and double tracked in the chorus.

Unfortunately, the Beatles' version (as well as one by Lenny Welch, which actually beat them to the marketplace by a month) had significantly different lyrics than subsequent versions by artists as disparate as Tony Bennett, Morgana King, and the Temptations. (In its history, the song has amassed over 200 covers.) Those who copied the Beatles' rendition skipped the poetry and left up for question whether or not the deliverer of the honey-flavored kiss returned to his first love as promised. Other artists were truer to the lyrics as well as the premise of the play. The movie definitively (if depressingly) clarified that the lover never came back and poor Jo went to her grave waiting for another one. According to Marlow, the Beatles felt the original version was "too English." "They asked permission to change it. As long as they paid me and gave no one else credit, I agreed," said Marlow.

Nevertheless, the original version's more realistic outcome was no doubt preferred by Tushingham fanatics like Stephen Morrissey, founder of the Smiths, who featured a scene from the movie in the video accompanying the group's first 45, "Hand in Glove," quoting from the script in his lyrics as well. McCartney, being just short of a true believer, borrowed a line from the script to serve as the title of his tune "Your Mother Should Know." But this was still a far cry from Morrissey's devotion; the play's author, Shelagh Delaney, is pictured on the record sleeve for the Smiths' single "Girlfriend in a Coma."

But the more comfortable narrative fit the Beatles' grand scheme (which was also Brian Epstein's) far better than the kitchen sink ethos of Delaney and the hedging rewrite. As opposed to the raw emotions and sloppy stage habits displayed by homegrown British rockers such as Billy Fury, Johnny Kidd, and Tommy Steele, the Beatles, under the tutelage of Epstein and Martin, dressed in suits and ties and were known to perform abject show tunes like "'Til There Was You" and traditional folk songs like "My Bonnie." (Researchers have thus far failed to dig up any version of "The Big Ship Sails on the Alley Alley Oh," the haunting final number from *A Taste of Honey*.)

All this may have brought them closer to their ultimate goal: the leaving of Liverpool and making it in America, but it also aligned them more squarely with the polished pop of the perennial superstar-in-waiting, Cliff Richard, and his backup band the Shadows.

While the Beatles appreciated Richard's relentless productivity (and the fact that he and the Shadows performed "Voice in the Wilderness" in *Expresso Bongo*, the excellent 1961 art house flick about Cliff's career), they had to be unnerved by his continued failure to dent the U.S. marketplace. By the end of 1962 he'd had nineteen Top 10 hits in the UK and none in the states, failing to capitalize on the Top 30 showing of "Living Doll" in 1959. They had no use for his backup band, either, although the Shadows, led by Hank Marvin, were quite popular under their own name, accounting for six Top 10 singles between 1960 and 1962, among them "Apache" and "Wonderful Land," none of which crossed over. That their influence was hard to escape is revealed by the fact that the first original Beatles song to be professionally recorded was a Shadows-like instrumental written by John and George in 1961 that was eventually titled "Cry for a Shadow" and released as the B side of "Why." It was the only time these two ever collaborated.

Ironically, after the Beatles' unsuccessful audition for Mike Smith at Decca Records, Brian Epstein paid Tony Meehan, former drummer for the Shadows, to produce the same fifteen-song Decca audition tape that wound up in front of George Martin a few months later. But there was no way the Beatles would continuing dressing up and dumbing down for Brian and George if they were destined to follow the same limited path as Cliff Richard. ☞

Things surely would have been different had they not been turned down by the coolest producer on the planet, Joe Meek, whose production of the appropriately spacey "Telstar" by his in-house band the Tornadoes (1962) was the second British single to top the American charts (coming just weeks after Acker Bilk's smooth instrumental "Stranger on the Shore"). As flaky and mercurial as Phil Spector, Meek was anything but meek in his dealings with the outside world, especially the musicians who fell under the sway of his power trip. But like Spector, he was forgiven his eventually lethal quirks (such as murdering his landlady before turning the gun on himself) because of his otherworldly talent. (Meek is known for accusing Spector of ripping him off.) Meek was the opposite of George Martin in every conceivable way except in his musical genius. He could segue from the skifflesque folk music of Lonnie Donegan (as the engineer on Donegan's "Cumberland Gap") to the outrageous antics of Screaming Lord Sutch, with room in his middle brain left over for tributes to Eddie Cochran and his ultimate idol, Buddy Holly. One of his acts, Emile Ford and the Checkmates, was the first black group to top the UK charts with the 1911 tune "What Do You Want to Make Those Eyes at Me For" in 1959.

R&B and skiffle credibility notwithstanding, it is doubtful that strong personalities such as Lennon and McCartney would have soldiered well in Meek's program for world domination. After all, aside from "Telstar," does anyone outside of England remember "Johnny Remember Me" by John Leyton, "Be Mine" by Lance Fortune, "Angela Jones" by Michael Cox (not to be confused with "Amanda Jones" by the Rolling Stones), "Just Like Eddie" by Heinz, "Tribute to Buddy Holly" by Mike Berry, or the entire oeuvre of the brassy belter Glenda Collins ("Baby It Hurts")? Even the Tornadoes' follow-up to "Telstar," "Ridin' the Wind," did miserably in the U.S., failing to climb past Number 62.

Few British singles were fortunate enough to cross over in those pre-Beatles days, especially into the Top 10. Lonnie Donegan, the King of Skiffle, did it twice: once in 1956 with "Rock Island Line" and again in 1961 with his biggest hit, "Does Your Chewing Gum Lose Its Flavor (On the Bedpost Overnight)." Quirky crooner Frank Ifield (an eventual Beatles label mate) struck gold in 1962 with his yodeling version of the Jimmy Dorsey hit "I Remember You," but received diminishing chart returns on three other remakes. Before their 1964 onslaught, the Beatles hit the invisible wall three times in 1963, with "Please Please Me," "From Me to You," and "She Loves You." American radio programmers were only slightly more favorable to Del Shannon's version of "From Me to You," which Shannon heard while playing a concert with the fellows that year. Although the record only peaked as high as Number 77, it was an important milestone nonetheless; the first Lennon and McCartney-penned tune to reach those shores. A couple of years later, Peter (the brother of Paul's girlfriend Jane Asher) and Gordon would take the Shannon composition "I Go to Pieces" into the American Top 10. By then the whole landscape had changed permanently.

After the Beatles hit it big, England broke wide open, becoming a market and a scene, a proving ground and a hotbed, supplying the American charts and audiences with a constant flow of quality material. For many years it seemed as if anyone with a British accent could get a record deal in the U.S., complete with a forty-city tour and several hit singles; anybody, that is, except for an act deemed hopelessly pre-Beatles, a list that was headed by Cliff Richard. (After almost twenty years in the business and several failed U.S. tours, Richard finally crashed the American Top 10 in 1976 with "Devil Woman," but by then it was too late to have made much of a difference.)

Billy Fury, England's second biggest male rock star, never came close, although he charted consistently in the UK from 1959 ("Maybe Tomorrow") to 1965 ("In Thoughts of You"). Fury's place in pre-Beatles history was secured in 1960 when he recorded the seminal British rock album *The Sound of Fury*, produced by Jack Good for Decca Records, and again in 2003 when a statue of him was erected at the Albert Dock in Liverpool. Intentionally meant to emulate the 1950s Memphis sound of Elvis Presley at Sun Records, the album featured ten tracks written by Fury and performed in a fury of immediacy by his studio band, which included the top British rock guitarist of the day, the smoking Joe Brown, doing his best impression of Scotty Moore. The leadoff track "That's Love" hit the Top 20. In tribute to Fury, (who had offered to hire the Silver Beatles, as they were then called, as a backup band, but was turned down when Lennon refused to fire Stu Sutcliffe), the Beatles were known to perform one of his American rockabilly favorites, Eddie Fontaine's "Nothin' Shakin.'" They also covered (courtesy of George Harrison) Joe Brown's arrangement of "The Sheik of Araby" as well as "A Picture of You," one of Brown's biggest hits. In 1974 Fury had a part in the well-regarded British movie *That'll Be the Day*, based on the life of John Lennon. Joe Brown sustained a significant career in show business for fifty years, remaining close to George Harrison and eventually securing an MBE of his own.

Tommy Steele, whose UK chart run peaked in 1957 with a Number One cover of the Guy Mitchell hit "Singing the Blues," was effectively finished as a recording artist by 1960, although he did manage to cross over to the U.S. in 1965 by landing a role in the Broadway musical *Half a Sixpence*. In the show, he played the role of Arthur Kipps, a simple orphan who inherits and then loses a fortune. After playing in over 500 performances, Steele easily segued into the 1967 movie version of the show, having already had experience as an old movie hand in the UK. (He played himself in 1957's *The Tommy Steele Story*.)

Other rockers of the era didn't fare nearly as well, including original Beatles mentor Tony Sheridan, for whom they eventually landed a gig as backup band in Hamburg, Germany. Sheridan had given them their first taste of recording (as the Beat Brothers) on the single "My Bonnie" (produced by Bert Kaempfert), which reached the Top 5 in Germany in 1961 (and the Top 30 in the U.S. three years later), surely upping their profile back home in Liverpool in the days just prior to Brian Epstein becoming their manager. Sheridan also had a significant stint working with noted English-born,

American-raised crackpot Vince Taylor and his band, the Play-boys. Oddly enough, both Taylor and Sheridan wound up being swallowed up by religious cults before their careers were through, with Sheridan taking the name Swami Probhu Sharan.

Not to be outdone in the crackpot department, David "Scream-ing Lord" Sutch claimed he was an Earl and ran for Parliament several times after his exemplary career in show biz tanked. But this was not before he graduated from the Joe Meek stable ("'Til the Following Night") into the clutches of a pre-Led Zeppelin Jim-my Page, with whom he collaborated on upwards of a half-dozen numbers, the best being "Flashing Lights." Page produced Sutch's 1970 album *Lord Sutch and Heavy Friends*, which included sidemen Jeff Beck, John Bonham, Nicky Hopkins, and Noel Redding. A screamer on the order of Screamin' Jay Hawkins, who was known for tunes like "All Black and Hairy," "Jack the Ripper," and "Mur-der in the Graveyard," Sutch had an act based more on costumery than musicality, making him a logical precursor to Alice Cooper.

Perhaps England's hardest rocker was Frederick Heath, who came to fame as Johnny Kidd in the heavy guitar trio Johnny Kidd and the Pirates. After breaking in with "Please Don't Touch" in 1959, Heath achieved immortality with his next hit, the Gene Vincent-inspired "Shakin' All Over," which reached the top of the British charts in 1960 and influenced a generation of rockers (if not the Beatles, then definitely their cohorts the Who, who covered the tune, as did the Guess Who, the Canadian band that launched their U.S. career with it in 1965). Kidd's biggest hit, "I'll Never Get Over You," came in 1963, the year before the flood of Merseybeat bands that started in the wake of the Beatles' success wiped out the market for such gritty sounds and sentiments. Three years later, Kidd died in a car crash.

The least explainable non-crossover to cross paths with the Beatles in the early sixties was Helen Shapiro, whose chart career peaked when she was seventeen after a magnificent three-year run, during which time she accounted for two huge international best sellers: "You Don't Know" (which never made the U.S. charts) and 1961's "Walkin' Back to Happiness" (which spent a grand total of one week at the bottom of the U.S. charts). The Beatles took Shapiro on tour, performed with her on TV, and wrote a song especially for her titled "Misery." But Helen's label and management (and probably Helen herself) agreed that the downcast lyrics did not fit her profile; hers was a much more empowering message than Jo's in *A Taste of Honey*. Thus, history was dropped into the lap of Kenny Lynch, whose recording of "Misery" made him the first artist to cover a Lennon and McCartney tune; not that it did him much good in the long (or the short) run. It fell to Cilla Black, former Cavern Club hat check girl and Brian Epstein protégé, to take the femme rock mantle from Helen Shapiro and wear it throughout the sixties, becoming the second most popular act in England after the Beatles.

But it would be unfair to cast Helen Shapiro as the Rita Tushingham of rock 'n' roll, although her inability to transcend the boundaries of her British existence is just as touching. She was never as waifish as lovely Rita anyway; never a shop girl like Jo. She was more on the order of a suburban pom-pom girl (sounding like a 35-year-old martini-swilling diva), more on the order of Lesley Gore-meets-Shirley Bassey. And she did quite well staying put, fashioning an outstanding career during which she crossed over (physically, if not saleswise) with 1963's LP *Helen in Nashville*.

Fats Waller, circa 1940s.

2

THE GREAT AMERICAN SONGBOOK

Paul McCartney's father was a musician who led a jazz band in the 1920s. John Lennon's mother taught John how to play the banjo and introduced him to Elvis Presley records. The mother of original drummer Pete Best ran a nightclub called the Casbah in the basement of their family home in Liverpool. None of the Beatles were casual music fans, even growing up. The music that coursed through their houses, mostly on the radio, but also perhaps on the *Black and White Minstrel Show* on TV spanned almost a century of songs. John Lennon's first composition "Hello Little Girl," written in 1958, has as one of its influences a song John's mother used to hum around the house when he was growing up called "Scatter-Brain," which was a big hit in 1939 for Frankie Masters, a moderate success for Benny Goodman (featuring Louise Tobin on vocal), and a favorite of jazz chanteuse Mildred Bailey. Although the two songs share little in common except a jaundiced view of women and their effect on men, it was this grounding in the Great American Songbook that would educate and separate the various Beatles from their more provincial peers on the Liverpool and, later, Hamburg rock scenes.

Starting out in musical life as a skiffle band the Quarrymen, the earliest incarnation of the Beatles, would only naturally feature in their repertoire a great old-time tune like "Puttin' on the Style," which enjoyed a 1957 run on the charts courtesy of skiffle king Lonnie Donegan, the Pete Seeger of the British folk revival. Donegan was partial to American folk songs by Leadbelly, the

Carter Family, and Woody Guthrie. The song, which was written in 1875, harkens back to the early days of country music. Vernon Dalhart, the light opera singer who became country music's first star, recorded it in 1925.

O f the myriad hits Vernon Dalhart (one of many aliases) accounted for on 184 different record labels during his career, "Puttin' on the Style" stands out as one of his more upbeat efforts. Although he established his musical identity by recording morbid ballads like "The Prisoner's Song," "The Wreck of the Old 97," and "The Death of Floyd Collins," here Dalhart dallies ostensibly in the realms of an old-time fiddling dance tune. Yet what's interesting about this is that out of all of the old-time fiddling dance tunes to choose from (not to mention the deathly serious Woody Guthrie and Leadbelly epics made available through Lonnie Donegan), on their very first day of singing together, both Lennon and McCartney were drawn to a lyric that good-naturedly critiqued the silly affectations of "the young folks." Even at this early stage of their partnership, the Lennon worldview was at play and Paul was focusing on the dance, with Lennon smiling as he inserted the knife.

Later on, while working as a backup band for Tony Sheridan, the individual Beatles, (including drummer Pete Best) may have had less of a say in their choice of material for their first professional recording session, produced by Bert Kaempfert, which resulted in the single "My Bonnie." This Scottish folk tune had been around forever and was constantly requested by the German sailors who flocked to the Top Ten Club to see Tony Sheridan. (It has been suggested that the Bonnie in question is Charles Edward Stuart, aka "Bonnie Prince Charlie.") The song's lone pop moment prior to this occurred in 1938, when a hit recording of it was made by the Scottish-born singer Ella Logan, more famous for her starring role in Broadway's *Finian's Rainbow*. But it's probable that if the other Beatles had any influence at all on their mercurial leader, they might have directed him to an arrangement by guitar virtuoso Duane Eddy, aka "The King of Twang." Eddy's rocking "Bonnie Came Back" was the B side of his 1959 UK single "Movin' n' Groovin'" as well as a crowd favorite at local soccer matches. It peaked on the U.S. charts at Number 26 early in 1960 (with the spelling of the flip side changed to "Moovin' n' Groovin'") and was included on the album $1,000,000 Worth of Twang, which came out at the end of the year, containing such eventual UK smashes as "Because They're Young" (Number 2) and "Forty Miles of Bad Road" (Number 11). Between 1959 and 1961 Eddy was all over the British charts, placing five songs in the Top 10. Whether it was George Harrison or Tony Sheridan who played the great guitar solo in the middle of the tune, it was no one but Duane Eddy who was being channeled. (On the Eddy track a nifty drum solo, probably played by Jimmy Troxel, replaced the guitar break.) "My Bonnie," as credited to Tony Sheridan and the Beat Brothers, sold over 100,000 copies in Germany in 1962 and hit the Top 5.

The Beatles got to perform four other songs with Sheridan at the Kaempfert sessions: "When the Saints Go Marching In" (which wound up as the B side of "My Bonnie," titled "The Saints"), "Nobody's Child" (a Hank Snow country hit from 1949), a knock-off of Chicago blues man Jimmy Reed's "Take Out Some Insurance on Me Baby," and the Sheridan composition "Why." As a bonus, they were allowed time to record two tracks under their own name, selecting the Lennon-Harrison original instrumental "Cry for a Shadow" and the evergreen "Ain't She Sweet." "Cry for a Shadow" was the B side of "Why" when it made the U.S. charts in 1964. "Ain't She Sweet" hit the Top 20 three months later, with "Nobody's Child" on the flip side.

The Beatles were big fans of the Weavers and Fats Domino, both of whom covered "When the Saints Go Marching In," and so they had to be thrilled to trot out their best Gene Vincent performance on "Ain't She Sweet." Long one of their idols, the gimpy Vincent had an odd predilection for dredging up ancient material from the heyday of Tin Pan Alley. During his checkered career he took on such moldy chestnuts as "By the Light of the Silvery Moon" (1910) as well as standards of a more recent vintage, including "Up a Lazy River" (1931), "Summertime" (1935), and "Pistol Packin' Mama" (1943). "Ain't She Sweet" (1927) came from Vincent's 1956 album,

IF YOU LIKE THE BEATLES . . .

Bluejean Bop, which also contained "Peg o' My Heart" (1913) and "That Old Gang of Mine" (1923). The Beatles were possibly listening when Vincent sang "Over the Rainbow," the soaring Judy Garland Oscar winner from *The Wizard of Oz* (1939) on his 1959 album, *Sounds Like Gene Vincent*, and immediately started including it in their live shows.

The Vincent pedigree alone was sometimes enough for a tune to make it into the Beatles' late night songbook. But on their ill-fated audition at Decca on January 1, 1962, the inclusion of four non-Vincent-endorsed standards has long troubled diehards, who blame this lapse on their manager, the square's square, Brian Epstein. Paul McCartney, for one, has gone to great pains to justify the band's genuine appreciation of such material, a prime example being "'Till There Was You," the key ballad from the Meredith Willson musical *The Music Man*. And while it's pretty hard to imagine any of the Beatles having the same kind of affinity for the show they may have had for *A Taste of Honey*, the claim that McCartney was introduced to it on a Peggy Lee album (played for him by a relative) rings only slightly truer. Nevertheless, McCartney certainly didn't shy away from singing it at as many important venues and in front of as many important people as he could, from the Queen of England to Ed Sullivan himself (they even included it on their first world tour, which kicked off in Copenhagen).

In later years, Paul put his money where his mouth was, going so far as to have MPL Communications, his publishing company, purchase the entire Meredith Willson catalog (joining works by Buddy Holly), which included "76 Trombones," "It's Beginning to Look a Lot Like Christmas," and "Banners and Bonnets" (the theme of the Salvation Army).

Similarly, it is unlikely that McCartney or any of the other Beatles heard "September in the Rain" on a Peggy Lee album, although Lee did perform it on radio in the 1940s, backed by her husband Dave Barbour's band. The biggest hit version of the song was Guy Lombardo's in 1937. More recently, R&B temptress Dinah Washington brought it back to the Top 10 in 1959. But the most likely source for the Beatles learning this tune is, in fact, Epstein, who was on record as having loved Washington's version. Moreover, it was also a favorite of his protégé, Cilla Black, who sang it on *The Ed Sullivan Show* in 1965.

The Beatles were also fans of the Coasters, the R&B novelty act that got much of their material from the stellar Brill Building duo, Jerry Leiber and Mike Stoller. As striving professionals in the songwriting trade, the ever upwardly mobile team of Lennon and McCartney found the careers of Leiber and Stoller greatly appealing. The Coasters were fond of the occasional standard themselves, having done an entire album of them in 1960, which included "Moonlight in Vermont," "Autumn Leaves," and "Satin Doll." Also released that year (although not on their album of standards) was the Latin makeout song "Besame Mucho," released as a single with "Besame Mucho, Part 2" on the B side. The Beatles were so enamored with this track that they led off their 1962 audition for EMI Records with their own version. The only thing that prevented the Beatles from owning the franchise on the cover was the sterling electric surf version released later that year by former Shadows bass player Jet Harris, which launched his solo career.

The fourth and final tune from the audition was nearer and dearer to their skiffle roots, "The Sheik of Araby," a slinky number published in 1921 that was apt to be found in the repertoires of American jug bands of the 1960s as well as the 1920s. The song also found favor among New Orleans jazz musicians, Fats Domino, and, in a strange bit of transmogrification, Cilla Black. Written to capitalize on Rudolph Valentino's silent classic *The Sheik*, it was sung at the Decca audition by George Harrison in response to a popular version by hot guitarist Joe Brown and the Bruvvers. It was eventually put out as a bootleg in England, paired with "September in the Rain" on the B side.

It wasn't only McCartney who professed a fondness for the golden oldies of Tin Pan Alley. When asked about the genesis of their early single "Please Please Me," John Lennon made a point of mentioning Bing Crosby's "Please" as a reference for its lyrical dexterity. This may have been less a case of him showing off his encyclopedic memory for random snatches of the music of his childhood (or, since "Please" dates back to 1932, his mother's teen years) than the more mundane probability that he'd recently heard yodeling balladeer Frank Ifield's version of the song, which was released as a single around that time. The Beatles also performed Ifield's signature number "I Remember You," which crossed over to the Top 10 in America just before the Beatles' arrival. Before that, it was a hit for Jimmy Dorsey in 1942, and prior to that, for Ada Jones in 1909. To return the favor, Ifield inadvertently punched the Beatles' ticket to America as well as his own. Chicago indie Vee-Jay Records, which had been known for R&B and gospel records, became interested in the pop field and signed a deal with EMI to license Ifield's music in the U.S. After the success of Ifield's "I Remember You," EMI attorney Paul Marshall recommended the Beatles' "Please Please Me" as EMI's next pop offering. The song wound up making the Top 40 in Chicago in 1963, the Beatles' first appearance on any American chart. Despite recording ancient standards during their early sessions, the Beatles exhibited a snarky attitude toward non-rock 'n' roll material. On a December 1963 edition of the popular British TV variety show *Morecambe and Wise*, they joined the hosts in a rollicking finale of "On Moonlight Bay," a number written in 1912 and updated more recently by Doris Day (the mortal opposite of Rita Tushingham). When they recorded "Three Coins in the Fountain" (made popular in the U.S. by the Four Aces) in 1963, they may have been thinking less of the 1954 Frank Sinatra UK chart topper than *The Goon Show* lampooning of it called "Three Goons in the Fountain." It's uncertain as to whether they performed either version of the song during one of two stints at the Three Coins club on Fountain Street in Manchester.

On *The Complete Beatles Home Recordings of 1963,* the Fab Four indulged in "Tammy," the Oscar-nominated song from the 1957 teen romance flick *Tammy and the Bachelor,* starring Debbie Reynolds as Tammy Tyree, Leslie Nielsen (later of *Police Story* fame) as the bachelor, and Walter Brennan as Grandpa. The film was hardly on the level of the gritty reality demonstrated by *A Taste of Honey,* and neither the movie nor the song by Debbie Reynolds could have been anywhere near and dear to the inmost hearts of even the least discriminating member of the group. Despite this, the Reynolds hit inspired a cover version by Duane Eddy, which appeared on his 1961 album *Girls, Girls, Girls*. Folkster Trini Lopez may have heard the Beatles sing it during the twenty-day day gig he shared with them at Paris' Olympia Theater in 1964, just before they left for America, since it shows up on his 1965 LP *The Love Album*. Debbie Reynolds' wispy rendition did have its charm, hitting Number Two in the UK in 1957, not the last case of a song far outliving the movie in which it made its debut.

Given the general pandemonium of their concert tours, with a set list pretty much fixed in stone from opening night onward, the best place to have heard the Beatles showcasing the breadth of their taste in the Great American Songbook would have been at a German nightclub in the early sixties (after hoisting a few cold ones). As with many a working band that came before them, the Beatles' sheer length and number of sets played in one night forced the lads to consult the grainier reaches of their memory banks at least once or twice before the evening's work was through. Thus, if you caught them on a good night, you might have heard them segue from giant to giant: from an Elvis B side to a Fats Waller novelty; from a Prohibition era shaker to a bow to the end of World War I, courtesy of the father of the electric guitar, Wisconsin's Les Paul.

"The World Is Waiting for the Sunrise" was written in 1919, one of many songs created at a time when an uplifting tone suggested that a new era of high spirits was about to commence.

Although technically not a true blue page in the Great American Songbook (since its authors, Eugene Lockhart and Ernest Seitz, hailed from Toronto), the song entered its epilog in 1922 through a hit recording by midwesterner Isham Jones and his dance band. In 1951 it made the Top 10 again, with a version by Les Paul, who made it a showcase for his vocalist-wife Mary Ford, featuring double-tracked vocals and his own incredibly slithery fretwork on his custom-made Gibson. Thereafter, it was picked up by facile guitar players like Chet Atkins and Carl Perkins, and in England, the Beatles' favorite, Joe Brown. On the 1985 TV special *Carl Perkins &*

Friends, George Harrison duets with Carl on the tune, although it's clear that George is only there to get a close-up view of his idol in action. Ringo joined the festivities, reuniting with George on stage for the first time since the seventies.

Considered historically comparable to the "Swinging Sixties," the "Roaring Twenties" was a flush post-war period of parties and prosperity, hampered only by Prohibition. The drug of choice in the twenties was alcohol (in the sixties it was grass and acid), with even casual imbibers viewed as outlaws in the eyes of the feds. If the Beatles were the leading edge of the rock revolution that marked the decadent youth culture in the sixties, jazz was the musical vehicle that was transporting the youth of the twenties into the ditch of moral decay. Sexual liberation abounded in both decades, with long-haired earth mother types sans brassieres freely cohabiting with their equally long-haired hippie consorts. In the twenties, cigarette-smoking flappers in clinging skirts stoked the lusts of otherwise buttoned-up young gentlemen. In both decades, dance was the key outlet for this pent-up sexual tension.

In the sixties, topless go-go dancers like San Francisco's Carol Doda burst forth from the confines of the repressed fifties to flaunt their wares in public. Doda's performance was a natural (or perhaps, silicone-enhanced) outgrowth of the twist, which earned its place in the decade's freedom-oriented ethos with an emphasis on each partner's solo gymnastic abilities as opposed to the rigid couples-only approach of the fox trot and the Lindy. In the late teens and early twenties the shimmy was the equivalent of the twist, representing a then-new low in commercial debauchery, almost the equal of jazz itself.

"I Wish I Could Shimmy Like My Sister Kate," (or "Sister Kate") was written in 1919 by jazz violinist A.J. Piron, either to celebrate the life of a murdered madam or as the progenitor of a sexy new dance craze. The song extolled the non-virtuous virtues of the symbolic Kate, who excelled at doing the latest dance sensation to sweep the nation. There are several contenders for the first racy lady to bring the shimmy to a mass audience. Much-married Polish actress Gilda Gray is known to have shimmied in front of

New York City sophisticates at the Winter Garden in 1919, the same year she brought the dance to Hollywood in *The Virtuous Vamp*. In 1922 she did it on Broadway in *Ziegfeld Follies of 1922*. Bee Palmer, an occasional singer with the New Orleans Rhythm Kings, probably did the shimmy to the group's "Shim-Me-Sha-Wobble," a number that combined the era's most popular dances: the shimmy, the shim sham, and the wobble. Palmer appeared as a chorus girl in *Ziegfeld Follies of 1918*. More notorious than either of those two was Mae West, whose image is on the sheet music edition of "Everybody Shimmies Now," which she sang in 1919 with Sophie Tucker. Seven years later, West wrote and starred in *Sex,* an experimental theater piece that played for a year until it was busted for obscenity. As a result, Mae was sentenced to a week in the slammer for corrupting the morals of the country's youth. She allegedly served her time wearing silk panties under her prison garb. Years later, Madonna (to say nothing of Lindsay Lohan) would take note. Although Madonna has yet to be jailed for any of her offenses, she did perpetrate a coffee table book of nude photographs of herself and others called *Sex*, which was published just before her album *Erotica* was released.

Long a hotbed of commercialized erotica, New Orleans welcomed Kate into the repertoires of some of its finest jazz musicians of the twenties, including Sidney Bechet, Henry "Red" Allen, Kid Ory, and King Oliver. It may have been publicly introduced in 1923 by blues singer Anna Jones, accompanied on stride piano by Fats Waller. In 1960, the Olympics, a California R&B group, recorded it as "Shimmy Like Kate," and during the Great American Folk Scare of the 1960s, it was again revamped by consummate folk picker Dave Van Ronk, the irrepressible Jim Kweskin sans the Jug Band, and Harvard bluesman Tom Rush.

Fats Waller, one of the ultimate showmen in musical history, outlasted the 1920s as well as the 1930s. With his impressive chops, a smile wide enough to reach the cheap seats, and notably droll lyrics, he was a worthy precursor of Louis Jordan and the jump blues that would jump start rock 'n' roll by the end of the 1940s. From Waller's massive repertoire, the Beatles chose the good-natured but sly "Your Feet's Too Big" (1939), which aptly showcased their superior taste as well as their equally superior fashion sense. (A few years later, Waller updated the premise in "Your Socks Don't Match.")

Widely covered in the U.S. and the UK (even Helen Shapiro had a crack at it), "Your Feet's Too Big," composed by Fred Fisher ("Peg o' My Heart"), was also a perfect fit for the repertoire of the Ink Spots, another important rock 'n' roll forerunner, whose mellow harmonies set the stage for doo-wop. Another famous song from the Fisher catalogue recorded by the Ink Spots was the noncharting "That's When Your Heartaches Begin," recorded in 1941. The song eventually found its way into the early repertoire of former gospel/country singer Elvis Presley, who recorded it in 1953 at the Sun studios in Memphis. The Beatles likely heard it when the Presley camp released it as the B side of his tenth million seller "All Shook Up," which topped the UK charts for seven weeks in 1957 while also hitting the R&B charts. But Elvis, despite being a walking Great American Songbook himself, gave the Beatles much more than a sneer and a ducktail to look at when they began contemplating their career in earnest in the late fifties and early sixties.

Eddie Cochran, circa late 1950s.

3

ROCKABILLY

In 1955 and 1956, rockabilly and rock 'n' roll were one and the same. Their moves, grooves, attitudes, outfits, and sounds were synonymous: loud, brash, self-destructive, anti-establishment, and a pie-in-the-face (if not a fist-in-the-face) to tradition. But tradition has been traditionally a worthy opponent against the forces of change (or at least the forces of youth). There is a myth that explains how the Beatles got their name from the 1953 renegade biker film *The Wild One* (starring Marlon Brando) in which a rival gang led by Lee Marvin is called the Beetles. (But the Beatles could not have seen the film since it was banned in the UK until 1967.) The point, however, is well taken. Youth is ever resourceful in its age-old battle against authority; black market discs prevailed in the underground, why not black market movies? The 1956 film *Blackboard Jungle*, however, was not banned in the UK, although city fathers and mothers probably wished it had been, after it opened in England, with Bill Haley's "Rock Around the Clock" blaring its incendiary call to arms. The song featured an iconic guitar solo by twenty-one-dollar-a-day session man Danny Cedrone, who first played it on Haley's 1952 recording of "Rock the Joint." In Britain, Teddy Boys danced in the aisles during film showings and rioted in the streets afterwards. Rockabilly had arrived.

By 1960, as sappy teen idol Bobby Rydell hit the Top 20 in Britain with a lame song called "Wild One," rock 'n' roll and rockabilly had long since started to separate, with one adding aftershave, a skinny tie, Brylcreem, a string section, a deferential attitude toward adults, and a taste for standards, and the other defiantly defending the Alamo of its lonely preferences where they could be surrounded and eliminated, one by one.

After several years of failed singles, brothers Johnny and Dorsey Burnette, founders of the Rock 'n Roll Trio, had a falling out and broke up their band. As a solo artist, Johnny sweetened his sound, cleaned up his act, and for his troubles was rewarded with "You're Sixteen," which went to Number 4 in England in 1961. Three years later, his fishing boat was rammed by a cabin cruiser in California and Johnny drowned. He was 30. Meticulous in their choice of live material, the Beatles covered Johnny's "Lonesome Tears in My Eyes," a Rock 'n Roll Trio tune from 1957 co-written by Dorsey, guitarist Paul Burlison, and Al Mortimer. In 1969 John and Paul borrowed the song's lead guitar break and used it on "The Ballad of John and Yoko." Once he was set free from Beatle obligations, the 34-year old Ringo Starr paid tribute to Johnny in 1974 with an unseemly version of "You're Sixteen," which topped the charts in America and made number 4 in the UK.

Gene Vincent survived several accidents in his short lifetime, including one in England in 1960 that killed rockabilly idol Eddie Cochran, and a motorcycle spill in Korea while serving in the Navy, which left him with a limp. Cochran was twenty-two and was finishing up a tour of England and preparing to return to Los Angeles where he was to be married to songwriter Sharon Sheeley (who was also injured in the wreck along with Vincent). After influencing a host of British rockers including Tommy Steele and Billy Fury, Vincent settled in England in the sixties. In 1971 he died at age thirty-six after tripping at his mother's house and rupturing a bleeding ulcer. Vincent was known for his taste for standards; five of the ten cuts on his first album were evergreens, making it acceptable for the Beatles to stretch in that direction. They would record Vincent's Top 10 hit "Be Bop a Lula" as well as its follow-up, "Bluejean Bop." A John Lennon favorite, "Be Bop a Lula" was the first track on Lennon's 1975 album *Rock and Roll* and one of the songs he was playing on the day he was introduced to Paul McCartney, who, in turn, showed him Eddie Cochran's "Twenty

Flight Rock," which Paul would set down on his 1988 album *Back in the USSR*. The next year, Paul recorded "Be Bop a Lula" for his acoustic album *Unplugged*.

Roy Orbison, who was a big influence on the Beatles' second single "Please Please Me," toured the UK with the group in 1963 just prior to his world turning black. Possessing a plaintive, operatic upper register, Orbison was a melancholy figure who married his teenage bride Claudette Frady in 1957. Although they divorced in 1964, they remarried the following year. In 1966 Claudette died instantly after her motorcycle was hit by a truck. Two years later, while he was out on the road, Orbison's Tennessee home burned down with two of his children inside. Haunted, Orbison made it to fifty-two, succumbing to a heart attack shortly after re-conquering the charts with a new hit single ("You Got It") and rejuvenating his career as a member of the super group the Traveling Wilburys, along with Tom Petty, Jeff Lynne, Bob Dylan, and George Harrison.

In 1959 twenty-two year old Buddy Holly died in a plane crash along with the Big Bopper and Ritchie Valens. It was a tragedy; it was the lifestyle; but it also became part of the legend. In 1954 thirty-three-year-old guitarist Danny Cedrone fell down a flight of stairs while possibly in the throes of a heart attack and died of a broken neck, just ten days after recording "Rock Around the Clock" with Bill Haley. Eight months later, *Blackboard Jungle* was released, which would have made Cedrone a hero. In 1956 Carl Perkins, riding high on the success of "Blue Suede Shoes," was on his way to appear on *The Perry Como Show* when he nearly drowned in a car crash that critically injured his brother Jay. (Jay would die from a brain tumor two years later.) Although alcohol wasn't involved most of the time, rockabilly cats feasted on their hard-drinking image; it was just a consequence of life on the road.

Although his career was derailed by the timing of the accident, Perkins survived and eventually made a tour of England in 1964. He backed off a bit from rockabilly, joined Johnny Cash's band, and became a forerunner of the rougher, tougher "outlaw" country music movement. Perkins lasted till the ripe old age of sixty-five, becoming a rockabilly guitar/songwriting guru for George Harrison as well as Paul McCartney. Ringo Starr's vocal spotlight on the album *Beatles for Sale* (*Beatles '65* in the U.S.) was "Honey Don't," the B side of Perkins' "Blue Suede Shoes." (When "Honey Don't" first entered the Beatles' repertoire in 1962, it was sung by John Lennon.) Ringo also recorded Perkins' "Sure to Fall" and "Honey Don't" on subsequent solo albums. In 1969 John sang "Blue Suede Shoes" with the Plastic Ono Band when he was moonlighting on the Beatles in Toronto. In all, the Beatles covered ten songs associated with Carl, second only to the twelve they covered by Chuck Berry; besides "Blue Suede Shoes" and "Honey Don't," the others were "Matchbox," "Everybody's Trying to Be My Baby," "Sure to Fall," "Sawdust Dance Floor," "Tennessee," "Glad All Over," "Lend Me Your Comb," and "Your True Love."

They only covered one song by Eddie Fontaine, the rousing "Nothin' Shakin'" from 1958, his only hit. In 1965, after appearing in several movies including *The Girl Can't Help It* with Jayne Mansfield and Little Richard, Fontaine was tried and convicted of hiring someone to murder his wife. Born Brian Holden, Vince Taylor went to Hollywood High, moved to London, then Paris, strewing rockabilly identities like false credit cards. At one time Vince Taylor and the Playboys contained Tony Sheridan in their ranks. It is debatable whether Taylor influenced Sheridan and how much Sheridan influenced the Beatles when they were his backing band, but all were on the scene together, drinking from the same tap. In Paris at the end of 1963, Taylor cut a single with "Memphis, Tennessee" on one side and "A Shot of Rhythm and Blues" on the other, two tracks the Beatles favored. ☞

Soon after Ritchie Valens went down in an Iowa cornfield, Tex-Mex rocker Chan Romero was cloning him much in the same way Bobby Vee and Tommy Roe were cloning Buddy Holly. Romero's manager (who may have been Valens' mother) even went so far as to approach Valens' label with his demos. Out of this ploy came "Hippy Hippy Shake" in 1962, a single that found its way overseas, where it was adopted by a bunch of bands, most notably the Beatles. It was then co-opted by another Liverpool group, the Swinging Blue Jeans, who had a transatlantic hit with it in 1964, breaking into the Top 5 in England. As their fame ascended and they were asked to judge an episode of the popular UK TV show *Jukebox Jury* on December 7, 1963, among the records the four Beatles were asked to critique was that very same version of "Hippy Hippy Shake." They eventually gave it four thumbs up, but with slightly grudging commentary. "I like the Bill Harry version," said John. "We used to do it," George acknowledged. "Good, but not as good as Chan Romero," said Ringo. "Nobody remembers Chan Romero," added Paul.

When last seen, Romero was singing Christian music. The Swinging Blue Jeans (or at least singer Ray Ennis) spent the next fifty years dining out on that song on the oldies circuit.

The Beatles modeled their harmonies on records by the Everly Brothers, and although they covered three of the Everlys' biggest hits in their early sets ("Bye Bye Love," "Wake Up Little Susie," and "Cathy's Clown"), it was the more obscure "So How Come (No One Loves Me)" that they performed live on the BBC, with the rarely heard harmonizing team of George and John. They found this rather lackluster track (with its historically inaccurate message) on the 1960 album *A Date with the Everly Brothers*, bypassing more obvious material like the Little Richard rocker "Lucille" and the monster rock ballad "Love Hurts."

In a couple of years, those sentiments would, ironically, be more than apt for the Everly Brothers themselves. After fourteen Top 10 records in the U.S. between 1957 and 1962, they couldn't buy another hit in America for 30 years. (They survived somewhat longer in England, with the U.S. stiff, "The Price of Love," their last Top 10 item, coming in 1965.) The Everlys hit the UK Top 40 a few times through the end of 1967 with "I'll Never Get over You," "Love Is Strange," and "It's My Time." In 1973, *Two Yanks in England* reflected their conversion to all things British, with a cover of Manfred Mann's "Pretty Flamingo" and seven tracks written by

L. Ransford, a pseudonym for the Hollies (Graham Nash, Allan Clarke, and Tony Hicks), which included the standout "So Lonely."

By then, both brothers were addicted to speed and Don had suffered a nervous breakdown. It all fell apart at a 1973 concert at California's Knott's Berry Farm when Phil smashed his guitar during a set before stalking off the stage. This was no tribute to Pete Townshend or Jimi Hendrix; it was the beginning of a ten-year period when Don and Phil were no longer on speaking terms with each other.

But the musicians who loved them, especially those in England, wouldn't let the legendary brothers fade into dysfunctional obscurity. In 1984 a reunion concert at the Royal Albert Hall was miraculously pulled off, breaking the ice at last. The album *EB 84* resulted, with the leadoff track "On the Wings of a Nightingale," a chart single written by Paul McCartney, some kind of a nightingale indeed.

By these fast and loose standards, Elvis Presley's ride from fame to fortune has to be considered nearly exemplary, if not virtually domesticated. Long since revealed in his many biographies as a simple good old boy trapped in a Graceland not entirely of his own making, Elvis was nonetheless extremely sensitive, insecure, and competitive about his place in the rock 'n' roll scheme of things.

While Carl Perkins lay in a near coma in a New York City hospital, Scotty Moore, Bill Black, and D. J. Fontana, in town for a gig with Elvis, came to call, bearing Elvis's good wishes. But no Elvis. Weeks later he sent a telegram wishing Perkins a speedy recovery. Did he harbor a secret grudge that Carl's version of "Blue Suede Shoes" had outpaced his own on the charts? Who knows? But is it a coincidence that Elvis never recorded another Carl Perkins song?

When the Beatles finally met the King in the summer of 1965, they were both ensconced in their respective huge Los Angeles mansions, like two pop cultural ships in the night, one bound for glory, the other headed for a reef in the middle of the North Atlantic. It had to have been a tense, stilted afternoon. Whereas a year earlier, Bob Dylan had famously turned them on to pot, Elvis apparently didn't offer them so much as a peanut butter and banana sandwich.

On the other hand, the lads were probably already stoned when they arrived and Elvis may have been loaded on a cocktail of barbiturates. The Memphis Mafia was there, all of Elvis's childhood pals. The color TV was on with the sound off; Muddy Waters was on the stereo. The Beatles played pool with Elvis's bodyguards. Elvis played some bass and the fellows eventually jammed and talked gear. Priscilla stopped by to curtsy like a proper hausfrau. Elvis had met her when he was twenty-five and she, fourteen. They didn't marry until 1967 after she turned twenty-one. On their way out the door, the Beatles were given souvenir holsters.

This was the shell of a husk that Presley had become, a brooding recluse reduced to making movies for the money and then sitting at home making fun of them on TV with the sound off. He had suffered through a drought of twenty-two straight singles without having a Number One hit. It had been three-and-a-half years since "Good Luck Charm" in 1962.

There are many quotes about the astounding effect Elvis had on people upon hearing his records for the very first time. For most, it was like a door or a window opening, the earth itself opening up to a new day, a new order. Suddenly, blind men could see; frigid women got all tingly; people went out and bought guitars; sideburns started appearing underneath the ears of otherwise ordinary clods in corduroys. Elvis turned people on to the previously hidden exotic worlds of R&B and country music, which often appeared on opposite sides of his 45s. His first single in 1954 featured "That's All Right," a song from the repertoire of blues man Arthur "Big Boy" Crudup, with the flip side, "Blue Moon of Kentucky," coming from bluegrass legend Bill Monroe. (McCartney paid homage to "Blue Moon of Kentucky" on his 1991 acoustic album *Unplugged*.) Presley's last Sun single repeated the pattern, with Little Junior Parker's scorching "Mystery Train" paired with "I Forgot to Remember to Forget," a country rocker co-written by Charlie Feathers. The latter song was performed live by the Beatles on the BBC. Elvis' fourth Sun single, "Baby Let's Play House," was an early favorite of the Quarrymen. Paul McCartney stated that "In Spite of All the Danger," the first original song recorded by the Quarrymen, was influenced by Elvis. On his acoustic album, Paul played tribute to Elvis's second Sun single, R&B great Roy Brown's "Good Rockin' Tonight." "Hound Dog" found its way into John Lennon's 1972 Madison Square Garden concert performance. As late as 1999, McCartney was still channeling Presley, recording "Party," from the 1957 movie *Loving You*, on his album *Run Devil Run*. The track became a big hit in the UK that year, whereas Wanda Jackson, rockabilly's only certified wild woman for a painfully brief time, had a U.S. hit with the song in 1960. Carl Perkins's version of "Blue Suede Shoes" also succumbed to Elvis mania, with Elvis's version breaking the Top 10 in England and Carl's nowhere to be found. British kids had a slightly different Elvis experience than American teens, as "Paralyzed," "King Creole," "A Mess of Blues," "Girl of My Best Friend," and especially the Bert Kaempfert-penned "Wooden Heart" enjoyed hit status in the UK, while in the U.S. they either stalled at the bottom of the charts or were not released as singles at all.

In 1965 you could forgive Elvis if in the midst of that dry spell all he really wanted to do was kick back with his pals and live off his legend and his royalties. His manager, Colonel Tom Parker, would of course not allow this. Like Brian Epstein, the Colonel had his gaze fixed firmly on the horizon. When confronted with Elvis going through the motions on "Kiss Me Quick," which they reviewed on their guest-starring stint on *Juke Box Jury* in December 1963, the Beatles had to be honest. "The last few years Elvis has been going down the nick," said Ringo. "I like his voice," said Paul. "What I don't like are his songs." "Elvis is great," echoed George. "His songs are rubbish."

Perhaps word of their critiques had reached Elvis by the time they had their summit a year-and-a-half later.

The irony is that Elvis was only dogging it, laying low, and playing possum until this Beatles thing died out. He'd withstood folk rock, hadn't he? Surf music? He preferred Hawaiian numbers, gospel music, Christmas songs, and tunes from his own movies, such as "Do the Clam," "Puppet on a String," and "Your Time Hasn't Come Yet Baby." By 1969 his ship turned around and headed back to Memphis, while it was the Beatles who were heading for divorce court. Starting with his 1968 TV special, Elvis found his voice, soaring on "If I Can Dream" and "Memories." He also found the top of the charts in 1969 when "Suspicious Minds" hit Number One, one month after the whole youth culture united under the peace signs of Woodstock. Feeling particularly confident at this time, he even recorded a couple of Beatles tunes for the first time, cutting "Hey Jude" in Memphis (1969) and "Yesterday" at a Las Vegas concert (1970). But his memory was apparently a lot stronger than his confidence. He didn't release "Hey Jude" until 1971, after the Beatles had safely broken up, a kind of belated get-well card to the lads.

Little Richard, circa 1950s.

4

R&B

As opposed to their encounter with Elvis, the Beatles' first meeting with their other main early idol, Little Richard, was a lot more productive. Having heard him on record in the 1950s, they joined him for two concert dates in England in October 1962. Forced back into rock 'n' roll by a hungry audience after an extended tour in the ministry, Richard shared a bill with the Beatles at Hamburg's Star Club during the first two weeks in November. He treated the boys to steaks, read from the Bible, introduced them to organist Billy Preston, and taught Paul how to sing his trademarked "woo," which he had learned from gospel singer Marion Williams, certainly a turning point in their history. A chalice had been passed.

If the Hamburg years were formative, the Little Richard chapter was climactic for the band. As perhaps the rock world's most incendiary performer, Little Richard influenced other incendiary types including James Brown and James Osterberg (Iggy Pop). He inspired one of the Beatles' signature live numbers, a mashup of Leiber and Stoller's "Kansas City" and "Hey-Hey-Hey-Hey!" (the B side of "Good Golly, Miss Molly"), which the lads learned after they heard Little Richard do it onstage in England. Two years later they brought it out of mothballs to open a last-minute show in Kansas City, bringing down the half-filled house (Municipal Stadium, home of the Kansas City A's, whose owner, Charles O. Finley, had booked the Beatles for the unprecedented sum of $150,000). "Long Tall Sally," the first of four Top 10 hits, was a song about an ugly girl in Richard's New Orleans neighborhood, covered by the Beatles on their second U.S. album. The song's original B side, "Slippin' and Slidin,'" was recorded by John Lennon on his 1975 album *Rock and Roll,* along with a medley of "Rip It Up" and "Ready Teddy," the last of Richard's 1956 hits. As performed by the Beatles, "Rip It Up" was part of a medley containing "Blue Suede Shoes" and Big Joe Turner's "Shake, Rattle and Roll." They also performed "Ooh My Soul," Richard's last Top 40 hit, from 1958.

At the end of 1958, Little Richard got his calling from above and abandoned rock 'n' roll for seminary school. With Elvis in the army, Buddy Holly in the ground, Chuck Berry fending off his impending incareration, Jerry Lee Lewis on the moral blacklist for marrying his underage cousin, Alan Freed on the payola hot seat, and everyone else having sold out to Dick Clark, rock 'n' roll in 1959 was on life support in the U.S., alive and well apparently only in England. Back in New Orleans, mystical melting pot of all things rhythmic, they hadn't yet gotten the word. Bumps Blackwell, Little Richard's producer at Specialty Records, was already grooming his replacement in the form of edgy bad boy Larry Williams. Williams's raucous style was particularly appealing to the Beatles, who recorded both sides of his 1958 single "Dizzy Miss Lizzy" (which found its way onto the *Help* album in 1965) and "Slow Down" (which they released as a single in 1964 and included on *Something New*). The album also contained Williams's semi-autobiographical "Bad Boy" as well as the "Kansas City / Hey-Hey-Hey-Hey!" medley. His first hit "Short Fat Fannie" and the album track "Peaches and Cream" were also Beatle favorites. ☞

Larry Williams was ultimately unable to withstand the curse of 1959. By the end of the year he had been dropped from his label, after being collared by police for dealing drugs. He spent 1960 in jail. Although they were sometimes rivals, Williams and Little Richard wound up working together, with Williams producing *The Explosive Little Richard* on OKeh in 1967, an album that was later dismissed by Richard as being "too Motown." Despite the Beatles' continued devotion to his music during their solo careers (John's "Bony Maronie" and Paul's "She Said Yeah"),

Williams' downward spiral continued. In the seventies, Williams was fighting with Richard over a drug debt when Williams pulled a gun. In 1980 Williams was found dead in L.A. of gunshot wounds—possibly self-inflicted, possibly not

The kingpin of all things New Orleans was Fats Domino, whose first crossover hit single "Ain't That a Shame" (in 1955 after a dozen R&B chart hits) made it into the early repertoire of the Quarrymen. It was the first song Julia Lennon taught her son John to play on the banjo. Domino's sixty-sixth and last chart single was a cover of the Beatles' "Lady Madonna," which spent two weeks on the charts in 1968. In 1975, Lennon recorded Domino's "Ain't That a Shame" for his *Rock and Roll* album.

The Beatles continued to mine one of rock's most fertile proving grounds when they picked up on Lee Dorsey's "Ya Ya," which was produced by Allen Toussaint. The lads recorded it with Tony Sheridan, and John Lennon would also include it on his *Rock and Roll* album.

From there, they diligently made their way through the rest of the history of R&B. "Some Other Guy" came from the New York City doo-wop streets of Chantels producer Richard Barrett. From Cincinnati came the Stereos' "I Really Love You," a record cherished by George Harrison until he released it as a single in 1981. Although the Beatles recorded the racy back alley blues of Little Willie John's "Leave My Kitten Alone," they preferred the white cover version by Johnny Preston. They sampled crooner Roy Hamilton by way of Elvis's version of "I'm Gonna Sit Right Down and Cry (Over You)." They were surely hip to early Ray Charles, favoring his 1950s R&B hits including "I Got a Woman" (1954), "Hallelujah I Love Her So" (1955), "Get on the Right Track Baby" (1958), and "What'd I Say" (1959). But they reserved a special place in their hearts and their repertoire for "Mister Moonlight," the B side of the 1961 single the eponymous "Dr. Feelgood" by the Georgia-born barrelhouse piano player Willie Perryman (also known as Piano Red).

In the evolution of black music and rock 'n' roll history, Hank Ballard's "The Twist" has been considered both a highlight and a lowlight, depending on who you talk to. The Beatles were in at the very start of the twist craze. Ironically, the song and dance that it inspired served to indelibly mark the Beatles' own transitional point in their career. Although Chubby Checker's version of "The Twist" reached Number One in the U.S. in 1960, Checker didn't even crack the UK's Top 100 favorite artists that year. In 1960 the fading old school still reigned, typified by Freddy Cannon, Bobby Rydell, Neil Sedaka, Brenda Lee, and Connie Francis, none of whom were at the moment twisting. Only later would Francis and Rydell try to cash in on the craze; Connie with an aimless album called *Do the Twist with Connie Francis* and Bobby collaborating with label mate Chubby Checker on *Bobby Rydell / Chubby Checker*.

By then it was almost 1962 and the whole Peppermint Lounge thing happened. The twist had made it to the cover of *Life* magazine, endorsed by Jackie O and Murray the K. It was the first baby boomer dance; a revolutionary sidestep and a blast of white noise for the organ-guitar- and-bass trio Joey Dee and the Starliters, who had a major success with "Peppermint Twist–Part 1." Dee's hit was written by Henry Glover, whose "Teardrops on Your Letter" was the A side of Hank Ballard's original version of "The Twist." Although Ballard never quarreled with the royalties he earned as the song's sole writer, he never achieved Checker's world-renowned status with the song. Checker's version of "The Twist" pulled off a rare feat—topping the charts twice; once in 1960, and the second time in 1962 when it even made the Top 10 in England. "People forget," Hank said, "when Chubby got hot, we got hot, too."

He was referring to his group the Midnighters, famous for salacious R&B hits of the mid-fifties such as "Work with Me Annie" and "Annie Had a Baby." Ballard's Midnighters had been on the circuit for years, but in 1960 they made the Top 10 with the singles "Finger Poppin' Time" and "Let's Go, Let's Go, Let's Go."

Ballard's quote could have referred to any act that adopted or co-opted the twist's insidious beat, a beat that would take over the American charts for the next two years, effectively washing the slate clean of all the well-scrubbed *American Bandstand* crooners stuck on the old-school moves of the Lindy and the stroll. The atmosphere was ripe for something new and fresh to emerge after the dancers had worn themselves out. At first this only meant Chubby Checker and Hank Ballard. Ballard had released the first version of "The Twist" a couple of weeks before Chubby lapped him, courtesy of his national exposure on Dick Clark's Saturday night TV show. Despite the success of Checker's cover, Hank's version still was able to crack the Top 30. In late 1960 Ballard released "The Hoochi Coochi Coo," which made it to Number 23. Six more dance titles hit the charts in 1961, including "The Float," "The Continental Walk," "Let's Go Again (Where We Went Last Night)," and "Keep on Dancing." His last charting record, in early 1962, asked the rhetorical question, "Do You Know How to Twist?"

A spokesman, if not an ambassador for the American music industry's practice of grinding a good thing into (gold) dust, Checker's plush 1961 started early when "The Hucklebuck" followed "The Twist" in October 1960. Then, in quick succession came "Pony Time," "Dance the Mess Around," "Let's Twist Again," "The Fly," the re-release of "The Twist," and "Twistin' U.S.A.," interrupted only by a Checker-Bobby Rydell duet on "Jingle Bell Rock." In 1962 Checker resumed where he had left off with "Slow Twistin'" (with Dee Dee Sharp), "La Paloma Twist," "Dancin' Party," "Limbo Rock," and "Popeye the Hitchhiker," interrupted only by the re-entry on the charts of "Jingle Bell Rock." But Chubby wasn't through. In 1963 he released "Let's Limbo Some More" and "Twist It Up" before switching gears from the twist to Bahamian folk songs.

By this time even Frank Sinatra had gotten in on the act, recording "Ev'rybody's Twistin'" while Count Basie came up with "The Basie Twist." Top songs in 1962 included "Mashed Potato Time" by Dee Dee Sharp, "The Wah Watusi" by the Orlons, "Dear Lady Twist" by Gary (U.S.) Bonds, "Twistin' the Night Away" by Sam Cooke, "Percolator (Twist)" by Billy Joe and the Checkmates, and "Soul Twist" by King Curtis.

It had become a national dance craze; the forerunner of disco.

Nowhere was the twist craze more rampant than in New York City, where Joey Dee and the Starliters became the house band to royalty at the newly-hip Peppermint Lounge on Forty-fifth Street near Broadway. Dee was a bit less hungry than some of his adversaries in the marketplace. After blazing his way to the top with the classic "Peppermint Twist–Part 1," he followed it up with "Hey Let's Twist," but didn't return to the Top 10 until he covered the Isley Brothers' "Shout–Part 1" the following month. Perhaps he was too busy making the movie *Hey Let's Twist*, which co-starred Alan Freed's favorite blonde bombshell Jo-Ann Campbell, but Dee wouldn't make it back to the Top 40 for another year when he cashed in with "Hot Pastrami with Mashed Potatoes–Part 1." (Dee's songs had a tendency to stretch out. If singles had had four sides, he could have filled them all.)

Originally recorded by the Phil Spector-produced Top Notes, "Shout" made the Top 50 in 1959 with a joyous, frenetic version by the Isley Brothers, arguably kick-starting the whole twisting trend. When the Beatles began performing "Shout" in Germany, they couldn't have known the tectonic shift about to commence, in music as well as of their generation. By the time they covered the Isleys' belated follow-up "Twist and Shout" in 1962, they might have had a clue. The Isleys' "Twist and Shout" hit the Top 20 in 1962, but the success of the Beatles' cover version resulted in its predecessor becoming all but forgotten.

When the Beatles' "Twist and Shout" was released in America, it went all the way to Number 2, as part of the group's 1964 chart onslaught. (In England, it even became the title of a 45 EP.) The record became a token, a memento, a throwback, and a fond farewell to an era irrevocably over. The era of the twist had been washed away by the tides, to be replaced for a while by the Beatles and only the Beatles, then by any band with a British accent, and finally by creative singers, songwriters, and bands on both sides of the Atlantic, leading the way to an unprecedented renaissance of rock 'n' roll music.

In Detroit, the renaissance had been going on since 1960, when Berry Gordy left the prize fighting ring to go after an even bigger prize. While Sun Records' Sam Phillips was famous for saying that he was looking for a white boy who could replicate the black sound, Gordy was polishing up a black sound and gearing it for a white audience. The result was Motown Records. Scouring the neighborhoods, high schools, filling stations, and his own back office for talent, Gordy's mission was to define the decade in black music. For his house band, he hired the best session men he knew, including Robert White on guitar, Bennie Benjamin on drums, and James Jamerson on bass, the aggregate becoming known as the Funk Brothers, a name ascribed by Benjamin. (Gordy detested the word "funk.") Motown's headquarters, which housed the recording studio, became known as Hitsville U.S.A. Gordy put his writers in cubicles and had them compete for the choicest assignments. He defined his goal quite clearly with the title of the label's first Top 40 hit: "Money (That's What I Want)" by Barrett Strong. The record was released in 1959 and peaked at Number 23 in February 1960.

The Beatles were quick to pick up on the record even though it wasn't a hit in England; at the time, Motown was merely a drain on Berry Gordy's limited bank account, but that would change in short order. Like most music freaks, the Beatles were avid record collectors, and since manager Brian Epstein owned Liverpool's popular NEMS record shop, it enabled them to sample new sides to their heart's content. The obvious message of "Money" appealed to all of them, but especially to John Lennon, easily the hungriest of the four. Very soon after hearing it, the Beatles added the song to their act. In 1963 they recorded it, using the song as the rousing closer to their second British album, *With the Beatles*.

Barrett Strong's Motown career as a songwriter flourished as he collaborated mainly with Norman Whitfield on a string of massive hits including "I Heard It Through the Grapevine" for Gladys Knight and the Pips and then Marvin Gaye, and "Cloud Nine," "Ball of Confusion," and "Papa Was a Rolling Stone" for the Temptations. By that time the sixties were over and Motown had become a franchise equal to that of the Beatles.

Perhaps the Beatles' favorite Motown artist was Smokey Robinson, as much a consummate singer, musician, producer, arranger, and songwriter as Paul or John. They loved the sound of his group the Miracles, whose recording of "Shop Around," co-written by Berry Gordy, became Motown's first Top 10 hit in December 1960. Their next big hit was "You've Really Got a Hold on Me," released in 1962. By that time Smokey had the chops and the confidence of the boss to write the whole song himself. He was already handling that chore for Mary Wells, writing two of her three 1962 hits, "Two Lovers" and "The One Who Really Loves You," while co-writing the third, "You Beat Me to the Punch" with guitarist Ronnie White. The Beatles adored Wells, Motown's first solo female hit maker, and took her on a tour of Europe in 1964. "You Really Got a Hold on Me" (with "You've" changed to "You") was included on the Beatles' second album. Ignoring all of the Miracles' hits and possibly with a hint of snobbery, John Lennon named "I've Been Good to You" (the B side of 1962's "What's So Good About Good-by") as the Beatles' favorite Miracles track.

Besides Mary Wells, Brenda Holloway was another Motown lady who toured with the Beatles, landing a prestigious opening slot during their 1965 U.S. tour. Holloway launched her Motown career in 1964 with the Top 20 hit "Every Little Bit Hurts." She is probably better known as the lead singer on the original 1967 version of "You've Made Me So Very Happy," which she co-wrote with her sister Patrice, Frank Wilson, and Berry Gordy. Although it was her last charting single, it became the first for the reconfigured jazz-rock group Blood, Sweat and Tears, whose version reached the top of the charts in 1969. In 1961 the feisty, streetwise Marvelettes provided Motown with its first Number One hit, "Please Mr. Postman," which the Beatles covered on their second album.

The Beatles had a soft spot for girl groups. The girl group phenomenon was a mini-trend transcending white and black artists, ranging from doo-wop to rock. It was largely a producer's medium, with Phil Spector at the reins of the Crystals and the Ronettes, Luther Dixon firmly in control of the Shirelles, Richard Barrett calling the signals for the Chantels, and Shadow Morton the wizard behind the Shangri-Las. Ronettes lead singer Veronica Bennett, who later married Spector (becoming Ronnie Spector), claimed that Phil's jealousy of the Beatles prevented her from joining the Ronettes when they toured the U.S. with the Beatles in 1966 U.S. tour. She did, however, tour with the Rolling Stones (the Stones opened for the Ronettes) and in 1971 recorded a single that flopped for Apple Records.

Although the Beatles were fans of all of the above, the songs they chose to cover came from the catalogs of some of the lesser-known girl groups, including "Chains" by the Cookies (Little Eva's backup band), "Keep Your Hands Off My Baby" by Little Eva herself, and "Devil in Her Heart" (changed from "Devil in His Heart") by a completely obscure girl group from Detroit called the Donays, whose records on the tiny Brent label George Harrison had discovered. Bypassed even by Motown, the Donays' record earned an improbable annuity for its author Richard Drapkin after the Beatles covered it.

Ever the iconoclast even in the girl-group realm, John claimed allegiance not to Rosie and the Originals' classic "Angel Baby," but to the song's B side, "Give Me Love," featuring a vocal by Bluford D. Wade, a San Diego R&B singer who was recruited for the session. Similarly, when the Beatles covered songs by the Shirelles, instead of the obvious choice "Baby It's You," they selected "Boys," the B side of the Shirelles' first Number One single "Will You Love Me Tomorrow." On their recording of the song (with a vocal by Ringo, his first on a Beatles disc) the song's female-oriented lyrics were ignored.

The girl group sound was a favorite of all of the Beatles, but one particular song had particularly daunting repercussions on George Harrison. In 1971 a lawsuit was filed charging Harrison with plagiarism for lifting the melody of the Chiffons' 1962 recording of "He's So Fine," written by Ronnie Mack, and using it in his 1970 Number One record "My Sweet Lord." In 1976 Harrison was found guilty of "subconsciously" copying the Chiffons' song. Damages weren't assessed until 1981, but by that time, Harrison's former manager Allen Klein had arranged to purchase the rights to "He's So Fine" from its publisher, Bright Tunes. (Ultimately, Harrison was able to acquire the song himself.) In 1975, the Chiffons, in the spirit of good fun, recorded their own version of "My Sweet Lord." Harrison, in turn, recorded "This Song," which satirically poked fun at the entire incident.

During his first visit to the U.S. in 1963 (visiting his sister Louise in Benton, Illinois), George stumbled onto an album by James Ray on the tiny Caprice label that included the recent hit "If You Gotta Make a Fool of Somebody." Ray was a homeless street singer who was living on a Washington, D.C. rooftop when he was discovered by songwriter Rudy Clark. Ray's story intrigued George, who brought the LP back to the Beatles. "If You Gotta Make a Fool of Somebody" made it into the group's repertoire, inspiring another British group, Freddie and the Dreamers, to record it. Their version made it into the Top 10 in the UK. In 1987, George recorded another song from Ray's album, "Got My Mind Set on You" (originally titled "I've Got My Mind Set on You"), which became his third Number One single. But this came too late for the diminutive Ray, who had succumbed to a drug overdose many years before.

John Lennon was probably responsible for introducing the band to the music of country soul pioneer and part-time bus driver Arthur Alexander. The Alabama native's first hit "You Better Move On" launched Rick Hall's Fame Studios in Muscle Shoals, which paved the way for soul music, a black alternative to Motown during the 1960s, led by stalwarts such as Otis Redding, Aretha Franklin, Wilson Pickett, and Joe Tex. The Rolling Stones nabbed "You Better Move On" and put it on their album *December's Children (And Everybody's)*. The Beatles settled for the B side, "A Shot of Rhythm and Blues," which became a staple of their live act along with both sides of Alexander's next single, "Where Have You Been (All My Life)" (written by the team of Barry Mann and Cynthia Weil) and "Soldier of Love." They recorded his third single, "Anna (Go to Him)," which was issued on their U.S. debut album *Introducing the Beatles* on Vee-Jay.

Like James Ray, Alexander also died before his reputation caught up with him, of a heart attack at age 53. Even so, his place in history is secure. In addition to the Beatles and the Stones, two of the other Four Horsemen of twentieth century rock also favored his work. Bob Dylan covered Alexander's very first single "Sally Sue Brown" on his 1988 album *Down in the Groove,* and Elvis Presley had a big hit with Dennis Linde's "Burning Love" in 1972, which Alexander had recorded the previous year.

Buddy Holly, 1958. (© BBC.)

5

THE SONGWRITERS

The package called the Beatles needed one more piece be-fore it could be presented to the music industry as something more than just another talented cover band: songwriting. In those days, and for the previous hundred years of mainstream pop music, there was more of a separation of church and state between songwriters and performers than would later be expected, if not tolerated. The Beatles' success as songwriters effected a tidal change in the nature of the process, relegating the pure songwriter to the sidelines and creating a requirement for songs to come from within a band itself. Before the Beatles, rock 'n' roll bands wrote the occasional song but mainly covered the hits of the day, whether that day occurred last week or twenty years ago. The Beatles had already distinguished themselves from the local pack by their exquisite taste in covering obscure B sides. But with the dawning of the sixties, it was time to take a closer look at what made good songs tick, and more importantly, who wrote them.

As collectors and connoisseurs, the Beatles were definitely aware of the tiny type printed underneath the title on a 45, which indicated the writer credits. Paul McCartney was probably aware of the publishing credits as well. So it comes as no surprise that the group's favorite songwriter of the era was Chuck Berry. What made Berry's songs different from those by Little Richard was that they were complete, well-crafted songs, able to exist apart from the performance, whether it was an onstage riot act or studio accident. A Little Richard song is inexorably linked with a Little Richard performance; it is hard to think of one without the other. Richard's songs were little more than vehicles for his vocal pyrotechnics, more often than not, of the screaming variety. But Chuck Berry's gift was so unique that dozens of his songs wound up becoming statements of a universal rock 'n' roll coming of age, fit to be sung by anyone wanting to touch that experience. The Beatles, of course, had dabbled in writing songs, with Paul in particular being fairly prolific. But these were, for the most part, perfunctory ditties that became as transitory as grade school crushes. Berry was the one who first put the idea of a song as a work of art into their heads. Surely it had been there already. The Great American Songbook was filled with the efforts of the Gershwins, Berlins, Porters, and Kerns of their parents' generation. But those were mainly theater writers who wrote for characters on the stage or screen. In Berry's world, the stage was a lot closer to the street, and the theater was all of teenage America. This was a vision the Beatles were eager to absorb.

Coming from a background in the blues, rooted in its structure, and a storyteller by nature, Berry understood the three-cornered triangle of rock 'n' roll's immediate antecedents— R&B, country music, and pop—better than anyone except Elvis Presley. And since Berry was a writer as well as a performer (and a mean guitarist), he was arguably at least as influential a figure (if not moreso) than Presley. His breakthrough 1955 hit "Maybellene" was based on a 1938 recording of "Ida Red" by western swing's Bob Wills. The song was a traditional fiddle tune that was covered a year later by *Grand Ole Opry* star Roy Acuff. Originally re-naming it "Ida May," Berry was instructed by label owner and producer Leonard Chess to contemporize the title. Berry's pianist Johnnie Johnson credits Chess with suggesting the name "Maybellene," after spying a mascara box on the floor of the studio. A former hairdresser himself, Berry was no particular fan of the song, but saw an opening and was not about to run away from it. "Maybellene" told of a hot chick and a hot car, two of the most enduring truisms in the teenage experience. Songwriting co-credit was initially given to Alan Freed and Russ Fratto, who helped promote the record, but their dubious contributions were eventually deleted from record labels. Although the Beatles never covered "Maybellene," Elvis Presley performed it on the popular *Louisiana Hayride* radio and television programs. It was also covered by rocker Gene Vincent, pop singer Tommy Sands, up-and-coming country star Marty Robbins (whose version was misspelled "Maybelline"), and wacky English rockabilly icon Vince Taylor.

The Beatles preferred "Memphis, Tennessee," a story of a divorced man who misses his four-year-old daughter, which they used at their ill-fated Decca Records audition in 1962. They especially liked Berry's songs that celebrated rock 'n' roll, such as "Roll Over, Beethoven," "Rock and Roll Music," and "Johnny B. Goode," the latter concerning a country boy similar to Berry himself who could play a guitar "just like ringing a bell." "Johnny B. Goode" was covered by one of the Beatles' favorite local bands, Joe Brown and the Bruvvers, as well as by Elvis, Buddy Holly, and Jerry Lee Lewis. They would share "Carol" with the Rolling Stones and "Too Much Monkey Business" with the Kinks (who also used "Beautiful Delilah" to kick off their debut album). With its frenetic wordplay and cynical worldview, "Too Much Monkey Business" was a song that set the stage for Bob Dylan's "Subterranean Homesick Blues" as well as Elvis Costello's "Pump It Up" and REM's "It's the End of the World as We Know It (and I Feel Fine)."

Rock 'n' roll icon Jerry Lee Lewis favored Berry's "No Particular Place to Go." His partner in crime, Elvis Presley, did a bravura job on "Promised Land." In England, the Animals went for "Around and Around" and "Memphis, Tennessee" on their debut album. The Stones did "Around and Around" on *12x5* and "I'm Talking About You" and "You Can't Catch Me" on *December's Children*. Rolling Stone bassist Bill Wyman included "You Never Can Tell" on his 2004 live album and DVD *Let the Good Times Roll*. John Lennon put "You Can't Catch Me" and "Sweet Little Sixteen" on his 1975 album *Rock and Roll* and the Yardbirds took on "Let It Rock."

Not surprisingly, the only American rock 'n' roll female to show a true affinity for the work of Chuck Berry was Wanda Jackson, who toured with Elvis during the late 1950s. True to her wild and wicked but perhaps partly manufactured persona, Wanda recorded

"Brown Eyed Handsome Man" for her 1961 album *Right or Wrong*. A recording of the song by Buddy Holly reached the Top 5 in the UK three years after the singer's death in a plane crash.

Holly had been a fixture on the British charts since "That'll Be the Day" hit Number One in 1957. An American original from Lubbock, Texas, Holly based the song on a catchphrase from the John Wayne movie *The Searchers*. After his death in 1959, Holly remained popular in England where eighteen sides made the charts, none of which came close to becoming a hit in the U.S. Included among these are some of his best, albeit overlooked classics, including "Peggy Sue Got Married," "Heartbeat," "True Love Ways," "Listen to Me," "Wishing," and "Love's Made a Fool of You."

The Beatles were aware of Holly from the very beginning. As the Quarrymen, their first amateur record in 1958 consisted of a version of "That'll Be the Day" backed with a McCartney-Harrison original titled "In Spite of All the Danger." Holly's acerbic attitude and horn-rimmed glasses appealed to John, and his uncanny melodic sense to Paul. If Chuck Berry taught them wordplay and storytelling, Holly taught them how to write a wrenching love song with a lonesome edge and a rockabilly twang, a sort of blending of Roy Orbison and the Everly Brothers. Plus, he had his own band, the Crickets. It was a package the lads found irresistible. They named themselves the Beatles in honor of Holly's group, with tunes like "Everyday," "It's So Easy," and "Maybe Baby" becoming staples in their nightly regimen. When they auditioned for Decca, one of the songs they performed was Holly's "Cryin', Waitin,' Hopin'," the B side of "Peggy Sue Got Married," one of his finest posthumous singles.

Only one Buddy Holly song appeared on a Beatles album, the haunting "Words of Love," which had flopped as a single for Buddy in 1957. It appears on *Beatles for Sale*, which was released in the UK in December 1964. (The Beatles also recorded the Holly B side "Mailman, Bring Me No More Blues" during the infamous 1969 *Get Back* sessions.) Over in England, Peter and Gordon were paying attention. In 1965 they released Holly's "True Love Ways" as a single, which made the Top 20.

Another Liverpool band, the Searchers, beat them both to the gate when they recorded Holly's "Listen to Me" in 1963 for their debut album *Sugar and Spice*. Fab friend and touring companion Jackie De Shannon, a pretty good writer herself, covered "Maybe Baby" early in her career. Another of the Beatles' favorite opening acts was Tommy Roe, who was virtually a Holly clone.

Bobby Vee also enjoyed a nice career based on the Holly sound. In the aftermath of Holly's death on February 3, 1959, the fifteen-year-old Vee and his band the Shadows filled in for the singer at Holly's next scheduled tour stop in Moorhead, Minnesota. This led to a recording contract with Soma Records and the release of Vee's first single, "Suzie Baby." In 1962 Vee recorded *Bobby Vee Meets the Crickets* with surviving members of Holly's band, on which he covered "Peggy Sue" and "Well . . . All Right."

Wanda Jackson put her own version of "It Doesn't Matter Anymore" on her 1959 album *Rockin' with Wanda*. This song, Holly's last U.S. hit, was written by Paul Anka, entering the charts three weeks after Holly's plane went down. "Well . . . All Right" and eleven other Holly tunes appear on *Skeeter Davis Sings Buddy Holly* (RCA Victor, 1967) on which Holly's Clear Lake bus mate, Waylon Jennings, plays guitar. In 2002, Connie Francis recorded *Connie Sings Buddy* for the UK Pye label.

English acts copied Holly less but appreciated him more. The Rolling Stones nabbed "Not Fade Away," the B side of "Oh Boy," for their first single; Freddie and the Dreamers put "It Doesn't Matter Anymore" and "Early in the Morning" on their first album; Johnny Kidd was a fan of "Oh Boy"; Billy Fury covered "Maybe Baby"; Herman's Hermit's performed "Heartbeat" on tour and put it on their second album; and the Hollies (who denied naming themselves after Holly) did an album of his songs as well. Cliff Richard and Peter and Gordon came late to the party, in some sense covering the Beatles covering Holly. Hank Marvin, Richard's guitarist in the Shadows, did an instrumental set of Holly cover tunes, and John Lennon put "Peggy Sue" on his *Rock and Roll* album.

But Paul McCartney had the last laugh on everyone. He bought Buddy Holly's song catalog.

While the Beatles respected not only performers who could write but writers like Holly who performed in their own bands, they did not scorn songwriters who punched a time clock, worked in cubicles, wrote on deadline, or went home on the subway to their husband or wife after work. They were hip to the Brill Building and everything it stood for.

The Brill Building was where many of the best songs in popular music history had been written; opening its doors at 1619 Broadway in 1931. When Tin Pan Alley relocated from Manhattan's mid-twenties to Broadway's forties, the Brill Building, located at Forty-ninth and Broadway, became the friendly confines into which generations of publishing companies came to occupy one- and two-man offices, living on top of each other, tenement style, much like early songwriters in the ghettos of the Lower East Side at the turn of the twentieth century. Amid its rattle and roll, neophytes and journeymen pitched their demos, often starting at the top floor and working their way down until they got a sale or hit the street. As the big band era gave way to R&B, early rock 'n' roll was foreshadowed by the likes of Jesse Stone, Charlie Singleton and Rosemary McCoy, Rudy Tombs, and others. Alan Freed had an office in the building. Elvis Presley had his publishing company here. Relocating to the Brill Building from Los Angeles were Jerry Leiber and Mike Stoller, who had "Hound Dog," "Jailhouse Rock," and the entire Coasters catalog in their back pockets. Former blues singer Doc Pomus, who wrote "Lonely Avenue" for Ray Charles, teamed up with Mort Shuman to write for the Drifters, Dion and the Belmonts, Jimmy Clanton, and Bobby Rydell. ☞

O nce we wrote two songs for Bobby Rydell," Doc Pomus told me. "His A&R man rejected one of them. Now, there was a rock and roll show and we went to it and Jimmy Clanton was working there. I told Jimmy, 'We wrote a song for you.' The song was originally titled 'Go Bobby Go,' so we changed it to 'Go Jimmy Go.' Somewhere there's a tape of Bobby Rydell singing 'Go Bobby Go.'

"I don't even remember writing 'Teenager in Love,' Doc said. "It was an assignment. We had a song that we'd already written called 'Teen-ager in Love' and Dion liked the lyric to it and wanted us to change the melody. So we changed the melody.

"I met John Lennon at a BMI dinner; in fact we spent the whole dinner together. One of the biggest kicks I had was when Lennon told me that one of the first songs the Beatles ever did was 'Lonely Avenue.' And he was telling me that originally all they wanted to do was reach a point, like Morty and myself or like Carole King and Gerry Goffin, where they could make enough money to survive writing songs."

Located a few blocks up Broadway, Don Kirshner's Aldon Music empire was considered synonymous with the Brill Building sound, housing some of the top songwriting teams in the business, among them Gerry Goffin and Carole King, whose first Number One was "Will You Love Me Tomorrow" by the Shirelles. Goffin himself was a devoted Chuck Berry fan. "I think Chuck Berry wrote the best lyrics to describe what it was like in teenage America in those days," Gerry said. "I think his was a more accurate picture than mine. I didn't realize how good his lyrics were until I got a job and had to write them every day."

Ironically, it was the success of the Beatles and their ingrown songwriting prowess that paved the way for a complete re-ordering of the hit making process. "First it was just sort of pop lyrics," said Goffin. "Then all of a sudden poetry got involved."

But it would be misleading to state that the coming of the Beatles immediately wiped out the writing community at the Brill Building. If anything, the Beatles and their contemporaries who followed their every move shined a light on New York City writers, much as they had re-introduced Chuck Berry to the rock and roll cognoscenti, along with Carl Perkins, Arthur Alexander, and Gene Vincent. Led by the Beatles' example, England became a vast new marketplace for tailor-made pop songs. The Beatles appreciated Goffin and King's slightly off-kilter, underappreciated sides, including "Chains" by the Cookies, which barely scraped the Top 20, and "Don't Ever Change," a Top 5 UK hit for the Crickets that never charted in the U.S. At their Decca audition they sang Bobby Vee's "Take Good Care of My Baby" and gave a shout to Goffin and King's babysitter Little Eva when they added "Keep Your Hands Off My Baby" to their act as well.

In 1964, at the height of Beatlemania, Herman's Hermits had a hit with Goffin and King's "I'm Into Something Good," which was originally recorded by Earl-Jean, a sister of one of the Cookies. Dusty Springfield broke through with "Wishin' and Hopin'," written by Burt Bacharach and Hal David; the magisterial Bacharach also wrote "Baby It's You" for the Shirelles with David's brother Mack and Shirelles producer Luther Dixon; Manfred Mann hit the Top 5 with the Jeff Barry / Ellie Greenwich tune "Do Wah Diddy Diddy," and the Animals went for the Barry Mann / Cynthia Weil classic "We Gotta Get Out of This Place." Herman's Hermits revived "Silhouettes," a Bob Crewe / Frank Slay tune much beloved by John Lennon that was once a hit for the Rays. Lennon said it influenced the writing of "No Reply." Peter and Gordon plucked Phil Spector's "To Know You Is to Love You" (made famous by the Teddy Bears as "To Know Him Is to Love Him") from a Beatles set list for their 1965 version, as they had done with Buddy Holly's "True Love Ways" a few months earlier.

The Searchers were especially partial to the Brill Building oeuvre. They broke through in England with "Sweets for My Sweet," a Pomus and Shuman hit for the Drifters. A year later they covered another one, "I Count the Tears." They did the Barry and Greenwich rocker "Da Doo Ron Ron," originally a hit for the Crystals. They took on the Bacharach and David tune "This Empty Place" right after Dionne Warwick was done with it. Their first hit was "Needles and Pins" in 1964, written by Sonny Bono and Jack Nitzsche, part of Phil Spector's Gold Star Studio team and introduced by Jackie De Shannon a year before. The Searchers returned the favor, bringing De Shannon's "When You Walk in the Room" to the Top 40 and later recording her "Can't Help Forgiving You." Their biggest hit was Leiber and Stoller's "Love Potion Number Nine," originally a hit for the Clovers. They came back with two more Leiber and Stoller numbers: "Some Other Guy," a longtime

Beatles favorite, and "Tricky Dicky," in addition to "Stand by Me," written by Leiber and Stoller with Ben E. King. Marianne Faithfull chose Jackie De Shannon's "Come and Stay with Me" as a follow-up to "As Tears Go By," penned by Mick Jagger and Keith Richards.

By 1964, the team of Leiber and Stoller, who virtually invented the rock 'n' roll sound the Beatles were weaned on, had just about run its course. They had by now been reduced to writing tepid movie songs for Elvis Presley like "Bossa Nova Baby" from *Fun in Acapulco* (1963). Covers of their "Spanish Harlem" and "Lucky Lips" by Cliff Richard (1962) weren't making it either. A posthumous take on "(You're So Square) Baby I Don't Care" featuring Buddy Holly flopped in the U.S. The Coasters, who the team had nurtured since they were the Robins in 1955, hadn't had a hit since 1961's "Little Egypt" (later covered by Elvis).

The Beatles had used "Searchin'" and "Three Cool Cats," (the B side of "Charlie Brown") at their Decca audition. They performed "Young Blood" on the BBC, "Some Other Guy" (originally a hit for Richard Barrett) at the Cavern Club, and "Ruby Baby" (the Drifters hit) with Tony Sheridan. They brought down the house with Little Richard's version of "Kansas City," especially when they played that Midwestern city. But by 1965 the Beatles were well into their own songs; in many minds, Lennon and McCartney had by now replaced Leiber and Stoller as the preeminent rock 'n' roll songwriting team in the business.

In 1965 Leiber and Stoller produced "Go Now" by Bessie Banks. (The Moody Blues would cover it later that year, launching their own career.) "Down Home Girl," a flop for Alvin Robinson, was covered by the Rolling Stones. (They had been running their own label, Red Bird Records, home to the ultimate New York City girl group the Shangri-Las, but in 1966 they sold their interest in it.) A symbol of their ennui came in 1969 when Peggy Lee's "Is That All There Is" became their last major hit, by which time Lennon and McCartney's own careers as a team was sputtering as well.

Roger Moore as James Bond, 1973. (© MGM/UA.)

6

GEORGE MARTIN

When the Beatles first met George Martin, no one could have been a more unlikely candidate to produce their records. At 36, he was nearly twice their ages. From his patrician upbringing to his choice of neckties, the Parlophone Records producer and talent scout had a style and stature that was diametrically opposed to the young Liverpudlian upstarts. But Martin and the erstwhile super group (especially John Lennon) clicked, partly because of a shared passion for the lunacy of the BBC's *The Goon Show.*

Martin's involvement with the Goons wasn't just as a fan and a devotee; he'd actually produced records for the Goons, including their classic album *The Bridge on the River Wye*, which spoofed the Academy Award-winning movie *The Bridge on the River Kwai.* Martin was a friend of Spike Milligan, the show's creative voice, who he met through Peter Sellers (whose early Parlophone albums Martin also produced). The breakout single from Sellers' second album was a parody of Lonnie Donegan's recording of "Puttin' on the Style," a nineteenth-century pop song that was in the early repertoire of the skiffle-mad Quarrymen. Later on, Sellers did one of the first covers of "A Hard Day's Night," performed in the style of Sir Laurence Olivier as Richard III.

The half-hour wacky weekly *Goon Show* had been a staple in sophisticated British households since its immaculate conception in 1951 and was a forerunner to an entire new wave of British comedy, inspiring Peter Cook and Dudley Moore to go *Beyond the Fringe.* (Martin produced their album as well in 1961.)

The affliction with the Goons immediately endeared Martin to John Lennon, who was just entering adolescence at the time the Goons took to the airwaves, and whose view of reality was inalterably shaped by their mind-expanding programs. The myriad sounds rattling around inside Spike Milligan's mind were accomplished through the insidious use of ingenious sound effects, engineered through a mastery of echo, reverb, multiple edits, and playing with recording tape speeds, all of which would become hallmarks of the Beatles' studio repertoire, and especially, John Lennon's mad, unspooling, and acid-soaked creative vision. To be a *Goon Show* freak turned out to an absolute requirement for producing the Beatles, as the group grew and changed, and as their studio techniques (and minds) expanded.

Ever since he came to Parlophone, George Martin had been cutting his teeth on comedy records. His earliest credits include Peter Ustinov's 1955 LP *Mock Mozart*, which involved fooling around with tape effects and overdubs. In addition to *Beyond the Fringe*, Martin recorded David Frost's satirical TV show *That Was the Week That Was*. He also directed shows at Peter Cook's trailblazing nightclub, the Establishment, where Australian jet-setter Dame Edna Everage (Barry Humphries) was known to perform alongside visiting U.S. personages like Lenny Bruce. Martin worked with satirists Michael Flanders and Donald Swann, who took on any and all subjects for their comedy songs (much as the droll, Harvard-educated Tom Lehrer did in the U.S.), producing their albums *At the Drop of a Hat* and its follow up, *At the Drop of Another Hat*. A rabid fan of the cinema, Martin worked with actress-singer Joan Sims, a regular in twenty-four *Carry On* films, and produced her two best-known singles: "Hurry Up Gran / Oh Not Again Ken" and "Spring Song / Men."

Martin's appreciation for comedy and studio wizardry may have found a kindred spirit in John Lennon, but his classical training (on piano and oboe) and fondness for film scores made an impression on the more tradition-minded Paul McCartney. As a fan of Johnny Dankworth's 1960 score for *Saturday Night and Sunday Morning* (another "kitchen sink" drama à la *A Taste of Honey*), Martin produced Dankworth's "Experiments with Mice," jazzy variations on "Three Blind Mice" that hit the Top 10 in the UK in 1956. In 1961 Dankworth wrote the theme for the popular British TV spy series *The Avengers*. That same year Martin produced Dankworth's first Numer One record, a version of the jazz standard "You're Driving Me Crazy," performed by a nine-piece trad band called the Temperance Seven, which featured vocalist Paul Macdowell. The Dankworth-Martin association continued in 1976, when Martin produced the album *Born on a Friday* for Dankworth's wife, jazz singer Cleo Laine.

Martin was equally adept at international folk music, producing the 1955 hit "The Bluebell Polka," by the prolific Scottish accordion player Jimmy Shand. Australian troubadour Rolf Harris had two Top 10 hits produced by Martin: "Sun Arise" and "Tie Me Kangaroo Down, Sport," the latter song crossing over to Number 3 in the U.S. in 1963. Martin's talents also extended to skiffle music, a British-born melding of jazz and traditional folk music. In 1957 he produced the Top 10 hit "Don't You Rock Me Daddy-O" for the Vipers, the predominant skiffle group of the era. (Years later, Paul McCartney would record one of their tunes, "No Other Baby," on his revival album, *Run Devil Run*.) At one time, the Vipers included Jet Harris and Tony Meehan, who along with guitarist Hank Marvin would achieve fame as Cliff Richard's band the Shadows, which would eventually move out of his shadow and go out on their own.

The Shadows' first hit was a cover of a 1954 instrumental written by Bert Weedon called "Apache" that had been recorded by another Martin artist named Jerry Lordan. Lordan's version failed to kick up much action, but in 1960 the Shadows' cover spent five weeks at Number One in the UK. In America, Danish guitarist Jorgen Ingmann's version reached Number Two the following year. (Lordan wrote another Number One record for the Shadows, "Wonderful Land.") When Harris and Meehan struck out on their own, they did so with Lordan's surf-sounding instrumental "Diamonds," which topped the UK charts for three weeks in 1963. The Beatles would also use "Diamonds" extensively in their live act.

The one blank on George Martin's resume was rock 'n' roll. He passed on Tommy Steele, which cost him a potential seven Top 10 records, preferring his backup band, the Vipers. To correct this mistake he signed Jim Dale, who quit the business to become a comic and then an actor after having one hit, "Be My Girl." Jerry Lordan became more successful as a writer. Martin's big signing of 1961, Shane Fenton and the Fentones, went bust after their lead singer died just after the group sent their audition tape to the BBC; in natural fashion, the BBC was oblivious to this and asked them to audition in person. The surviving group members decided to honor Fenton (at the request of his grieving mom) by not breaking up and recruited the band's roadie, Bernard Jewry, to assume the lead role at the audition. The audition was a success and in short order they were recording for EMI (which released a *Best of the Fentones* album in 2003). After their single "I'm a Moody Guy" hit the Top 20 in 1962, further singles like "Walk Away" and "It's All Over Now" failed to sustain their momentum. At the beginning of the next decade, Jewry (aka Shane Fenton II) became Alvin Stardust and achieved considerably more fame.

George Martin's track record showed that he was not just eclectic; he was an authority on a variety of musical styles in addition to being a schooled musician; hardly the empty corporate suit perceived by the gang of scruffy punks from Liverpool. What appealed to all of the Beatles initially was the simple fact that he was willing to sign them. As they were surprised to find out, Martin could also recognize a hit single when he heard one; however, this was not the case with the Beatles' first release. Martin favored a tune called "How Do You Do It?" a song that was written by Mitch Murray, whose collaborative efforts with Peter Callander would result in a string of hits for Merseybeat artists including Freddie and the Dreamers, Gerry and the Pacemakers, Cliff Richard and the Shadows, and Georgie Fame. The Beatles, on the other hand, were unanimously in favor of using their own song "Love Me Do."

As predisposed as the Beatles may have been to cooperate with this sophisticated authority figure, they were still cocky enough to trust their own instincts on matters musical. Brian Epstein was permitted to dress them in suits and ties and he also prevailed upon them to quit drinking and popping pills on stage. But when it came to issuing their first single, they drew the line. In addition to objecting to their choice of material, Martin found Ringo Starr wanting as a drummer, and had his own man Andy White in the wings, ready to sit in. In this case, the band relented. Although the first pressing of the single version of "Love Me Do" featured Ringo on drums, later editions, including the album version, included White on drums and Ringo on tambourine.

When it came time to record their second single a few weeks later, order was restored to the universe with the Orbison-Everly-Holly-inspired "Please Please Me," featuring John Lennon playing harmonica in a style he had picked up from Delbert McClinton ("Hey, Baby!"). Beginning with this record, Ringo played drums from then on. Martin had little to do but congratulate the team on what he accurately predicted would be their first Number One hit, a prediction that was born out on two UK music charts, although the record didn't reach the U.S. listings until the onslaught of Beatlemania in 1964.

But Martin didn't just sit in the dugout like the manager of the New York Yankees as the Beatles coasted to twenty-seven world championships. He still made most of the musical decisions, remaining in the middle of the scrum, and demonstrating his amazing versatility even after the Beatles started flexing their studio muscles and questioning every rule in the book. Martin had to, at one moment, keep up with a frantic John Lennon on Chuck Berry's "Rock and Roll" and convince Paul McCartney to employ a string quartet on "Yesterday" at another. On "Yellow Submarine," Martin was in his full *Goon Show* glory, with bells, whistles, chains, and tin cans galore in the foreground while John and Paul played Peter Sellers and Spike Milligan in the background. On "Tomorrow Never Knows," Martin and his brilliant engineer Geoff Emerick somehow managed to satisfy Lennon's request for the sound of a thousand Tibetan monks without going over budget. On "In My Life" he even pulled a baroque harpsichord sound out of his arsenal by speeding up a piano (playing it himself). For "Eleanor Rigby" he flexed his scoring chops, inspired by Bernard Hermann's *Psycho* to arrange an accompaniment for string octet. For another session, he brought in a French horn ("For No One"), and when McCartney heard David Mason play piccolo trumpet on a Royal Philharmonic Orchestra broadcast of Bach's "Brandenburg Concerto No. 2," Martin, who was friends with Mason, brought him in to overdub a solo on "Penny Lane." When John Lennon wanted specific sounds for "Strawberry Fields Forever" and "I Am the Walrus," Martin, without a second thought for his own safety, jumped inside of Lennon's acid-expanded mind, found what was rattling around in there, and made an arrangement of it.

After the Beatles broke up, Martin was preparing a score for the James Bond film *Live and Let Die* when an opportunity arose to write the opening title theme. Martin immediately called Paul McCartney, just as he had done with theme songs for other Bond films when he hired two other previous clients, Shirley Bassey ("Goldfinger") and Matt Monro ("From Russia with Love").

Brian Epstein saw to it that "How Do You Do It?" found a home with another of his clients, Gerry and the Pacemakers, whose version, also under George Martin's supervision, spent three weeks at Number One in 1963. Epstein kept Martin busy with his other main acts, Billy J. Kramer and the Dakotas and ex-hat check girl Cilla Black. Compared to the enormous, riveting, soap operatic changes of everyday life with the Beatles, however, producing these other acts was probably as interesting as sleepwalking to Martin. His association with middle-of-the-road crooner Matt Monro had to be equally humdrum. But Martin probably realized something of a career wet dream when in 1964 he got the chance to work with British singing legend Alma Cogan, producing her song "It's You." Although it wasn't a hit, Martin produced a pair of Beatle cover songs for her to record: "Eight Days a Week," one of her finest performances, and "Help!" which was on the B side. In return, Cogan befriended the Beatles and invited them to her lavish parties, giving them a taste of what lay in wait on the other side of a few more hit singles.

By the mid-sixties, drugs and intramural tensions were becoming more of an influence on the Beatles than Martin. But his leaving EMI was due to their failure to financially acknowledge his success with the Beatles. He then opened his own AIR studios. He still worked with his main clients on landmark achievements like the endlessly creative *Sgt. Pepper's Lonely Hearts Club Band*, but now he had another, slightly more prosperous revenue stream. The first act he signed there was a white R&B contingent called the Action, who were routinely mistaken for black due to their covers of tunes by the Temptations ("Since I Lost My Baby"), the Marvelettes ("I'll Keep Holding On"), and Bob and Earl ("Harlem Shuffle"). Martin next produced the duo of David and Jonathan (Roger Greenaway and Roger Cook), who would go on to write such classics as "Long Cool Woman (In a Black Dress)" for the Hollies and "I'd Like to Teach the World to Sing (In Perfect Harmony)" for the New Seekers. Under their own alias, the best they could come up with was the 1966 period piece "Lovers of the World Unite," which went to Number 7 in the UK. Ironically, their biggest hit was a cover of Lennon and McCartney's "Michelle," which made the Top 20 in the U.S.

In 1967 Martin's affinity for novelties asserted itself again with his production of the Ivor Cutler Trio's album *Ludo*, which featured such Goon-like titles like "Good Morning! How Are You? Shut Up!" and "A Suck of My Thumb." A favorite of John Lennon's, Ivor Cutler was aptly cast as Mr. Bloodvessel in the Beatles television film *Magical Mystery Tour*. During the protracted squabbles interrupted by the occasional bursts of genius that characterized "The White Album" and *Abbey Road*, Martin couldn't escape the Beatles connection. For a time, the Scaffold, a trio that included Paul McCartney's brother Mike (using the pseudonym Mike McGear), was the house band at the Establishment, a London nightclub co-founded by Peter Cook. (The Bonzo Dog Doo-Dah Band performed there as well.) The Scaffold had their first hit "Thank U Very Much" in 1968, followed by "Lily the Pink" (an adaptation of the folk song "The Ballad of Lydia Pinkham"), which went to Number One, aided and abetted by Jack Bruce on bass, and Elton John and Graham Nash on backing vocals. Between 1969 and 1971 Martin produced records by Edwards Hand, a Beatlesque group consisting of Rod Edwards and Roger Hand. Three albums resulted, including the eponymous *Edwards Hand*, which was followed by *Stranded* and *Rainshine*, achieving little more than a vision of Beatles lite.

After shepherding Ringo Starr's *Sentimental Journey*, a solo album of pop standards, to the marketplace in 1970, Martin continued along his eclectic way, with excursions into roots rock (Seatrain's *2nd Album* and *Marblehead Messenger*), new age (The Paul Winter Consort's *Icarus*), classical vocal harmonies (The King's Singers, whose repertoire ranged from eighteenth-century oratorios and Christmas songs to Flanders and Swann and Lennon-McCartney covers), to the most classical of jazz rock (*Apocalypse* by John McLaughlin and the Mahavishnu Orchestra, featuring Jean-Luc Ponty on violin and the London Symphony Orchestra, conducted by Michael Tilson Thomas).

In 1974 Martin took over producing records by America, a London-based trio of U.S. Air Force brats that had their first hit in 1971 with the Neil Young-influenced "A Horse with No Name." The song went to Number 3 in England, and a year later, it topped the U.S. charts. Three albums later, the group, consisting of Dewey Bunnell, Gerry Beckley, and Dan Peek, decided to go in a different direction and hired Martin, who added strings and brass to their next four albums: *Holiday, Hearts, Hideaway,* and *Harbor*. The result was a bunch of U.S. chart successes that included such Beatle-influenced hits as "Tin Man," "Sister Golden Hair," "Daisy Jane," and "Today's the Day." Ironically, none of these songs cracked the UK Top 40, illustrating perhaps the record-buying audience's desire to move on from the Beatlesque to something a little more reflective of those angry times. By 1977 the punk rock sound of the Damned, the Sex Pistols, and the Clash would be more to their liking.

Punk was not a sound that appealed to George Martin. He took refuge in the other dominant genre of the 1970s, arena-based heavy metal guitar-driven pyrotechnics. As tasteful as he was, he turned for his guitar fix to a master of the form, Jeff Beck. Originally with the seminal British heavy metal band the Yardbirds, which at one time also featured Jimmy Page and Eric Clapton, Beck had been fronting his own group since 1968's bluesy *Truth* (featuring Rod Stewart on lead vocals). With *Blow by Blow* (1974) and *Wired* (1975), he burnished his reputation as an instrumentalist by expanding into the realm of fusion. Standout tracks from *Blow by Blow* include Stevie Wonder's "Cause We've Ended as Lovers" and keyboardist Max Middleton's "Freeway Jam." Martin revived his arranging chops with stellar work on "Scatterbrain" (not the 1939 big band standard preferred by John Lennon's mom) and "Diamond Dust." And guess who suggested the Lennon and McCartney cover of "She's a Woman"? For *Wired*, Beck brought Jan Hammer and Narada Michael Walden in from the Mahavishnu Orchestra; the Charles Mingus classic "Goodbye Pork Pie Hat" would become a permanent part of Beck's repertoire.

Martin worked with three songwriters in the mid-to-late seventies, only one of whom broke through to performing artist glory. The group American Flyer was a quartet consisting of émigrés from other rock groups including Craig Fuller (Pure Prairie League), Steve Katz (Blood, Sweat and Tears), Doug Yule (Velvet Underground), and Eric Kaz (Blues Magoos). Kaz's signal claim to fame was the torch song "Love Has No Pride," which he co-wrote with Libby Titus. It was recorded by Bonnie Raitt (1972), Linda Ronstadt (1973), and Tracy Nelson (1974), but failed to transform American Flyer into anything more than a platform for future demos.

Jimmy Webb ("MacArthur Park," "Wichita Lineman," "Galveston," "By the Time I Get to Phoenix," and many others) was eagerly looking forward to following writers like Randy Newman and Leonard Cohen into the singer-songwriter niche, but an ill-conceived collection of his early demos released in 1968 was trashed by critics, thwarting his efforts. After an absence of three years, Webb emerged with his sixth album in 1977, titled *El Mirage*, which was produced by George Martin. With various superstars dropping in to lend support, Webb put together as fine a track list as ever, but still failed to cross over. A song from that album, "The

Highwayman," became a huge country hit for the super group of Willie Nelson, Waylon Jennings, Johnny Cash, and Kris Kristofferson, calling themselves the Highwaymen. (The name reflected their constant touring and outlaw spirit.) Webb's "The Moon's a Harsh Mistress" (named for a science fiction novel by Robert Heinlein) is one of his greatest songs; an especially haunting version was recorded by Linda Ronstadt. And any opportunity to hear his venerable gem "P. F. Sloan" again is a moment worth savoring.

Neil Sedaka started a successful singing career in the late 1950s under the tutelage of Brill Building baron (once removed to 1650 Broadway) Don Kirshner. But in 1963, after a four-year run on the Top 10 (about average for teen idols in those days), he was considered washed up at the age of 23. Undaunted, he continued to record, write, and tour the UK and Australia until 1971 when his top ten hit of 1959, "Oh! Carol" (written about Carole King, whose *Tapestry* LP was becoming a worldwide sensation) was reissued in the UK and he subsequently moved his family: lock, stock, and housekeeper Mary, to London. The albums *Emergence* and *Solitaire*, released in 1971 and 1972, respectively, started his comeback. In 1974, *Sedaka's Back* was released on Elton John's startup Rocket label (soon to be home to Kiki Dee). The album produced a Number One hit ("Laughter in the Rain") as well as the original version of the Sedaka-Greenfield composition "Love Will Keep Us Together," which hit Number One in 1975 as recorded by the Captain and Tennille. George Martin produced Sedaka's 1977 album *A Song*, which was recorded for Elektra. Although it was a classy affair, it yielded only one chart single, "Amarillo."

In the early 1980s Martin moved restlessly, recording hard rock (*No Place to Run* by UFO), arena rock (*All Shook Up* by Cheap Trick), pop-rock (*Time Exposure* by Little River Band), and new wave experimentalism (*Quartet* by Ultravox), at the same time reuniting with Paul McCartney on the landmark Grammy-nominated CD *Tug of War*. Begun toward the end of 1980, production on the album was interrupted for two months after the murder of John Lennon in New York City. *Tug of War*, which could have been a metaphor for both McCartney and Martin's Beatles experiences, features "Here

Today," Paul's tribute to John. Ringo Starr sat in on drums on the second track "Take It Away," which also featured Martin playing piano. The Beatles' longtime hero Carl Perkins was featured on "Get It," but the highlight of the album was undoubtedly Paul's duet with Stevie Wonder on "Ebony and Ivory," a song that topped the charts both in the U.S. and the UK.

Another indelible moment in a career studded with them occurred in 1997 when George Martin was brought in to produce an update to "Candle in the Wind," Elton John's response to the death of Diana, Princess of Wales in an automobile accident, with Bernie Taupin recrafting his original 1973 lyrics. Martin added a flutist and a string quartet to the arrangement, resulting in a record that became the best-selling single in UK history, with some thirty-three million copies sold worldwide, much of it during the record's first week of release. Although "Candle in the Wind" was originally written about tortured pop cultural icon Marilyn Monroe, it could easily have been attributed to the Beatles, George Martin's early discovery, another act whose flame burned briefly but brightly and whose legend will live forever.

Bob Dylan, circa 1960s. (© CBS, INC.)

7

FOLK ROCK

On August 28, 1964, the Beatles had the first of five meet-ings with Bob Dylan. The initial encounter took place at a suite in New York's Delmonico Hotel where the Beatles were staying. The Dylan summit was a good deal more casual than their first awkward encounter with Elvis Presley would be a year later. Dylan had misheard the lyrics to "I Want to Hold Your Hand" (thinking the phrase "I can't hide" was "I get high"), so when he casually passed John Lennon a joint, it was because he assumed that the Beatles were already into pot. Lennon quickly passed it to Ringo who defied druggy etiquette by smoking the entire joint instead of passing it on. It turned out that although they might have sampled a smoke or two in Hamburg, the Beatles preferred the old fashioned stuff: liquor and pills. Dylan took care of that lapse of hipness immediately, but it wouldn't be the first time in musical history that a slight misinterpretation resulted in the world changing. ☞

I think what initially attracted me to the Beatles was the fact that they were using folk changes," said Roger McGuinn, founder of the Byrds, in an interview I conducted. "I'd been listening to Bob Gibson, who used some pretty slick chord progressions for a folk singer. He used a lot of passing chords like the Beatles ended up doing. So when I heard the Beatles. I went, 'Oh, I love those changes.' I loved their harmonies of the fourths and fifths, which were also folk music kind of harmonies, like sea shanties. I think because they had been a skiffle band and because they came from where they did, that music was just in the air there. They were doing their version of the fifties rock 'n' roll/rockabilly sound and the folk thing combined. That's what it was. When I got to meet them, I found out they didn't know they were doing that. They didn't know how to fingerpick and they didn't play banjos or mandolins or anything. They weren't coming from where I was coming from at all, which I'd given them credit for. I thought they knew all that stuff and were just being real slick about it. But it was just kind of an accident. It was a great accident."

Folk rock was already being officially christened in the world outside the locked door of the Delmonico hotel room by the Animals, who had just sent "House of the Rising Sun" to the top of the UK chart and were in the process of doing the same in the U.S. with an arrangement cribbed from Dylan's first album. (Dylan, in turn, had borrowed it from Dave Van Ronk, the erstwhile "Mayor of MacDougal Street," who sometimes let Bob crash on his couch.) Roger McGuinn may have caught a whiff of a sea shanty when he heard "Baby's in Black" later in the year, but Lennon had already recorded what most people think of as his first Dylan-influenced song, "I'm a Loser," two weeks prior to the meeting at the Delmonico. The Beatles had been aware of Dylan ever since 1963, when George Harrison brought a copy of the *Freewheelin'* album to Paris for them all to sample. "I'm a Loser" was Dylanesque only in comparison to the less word-oriented songs Lennon and McCartney were accustomed to writing. Although the Beatles had already begun the process of reinventing popular music structures, they were still hungering for something more substantial, both musically as well as lyrically. As the leading edge and voice of his generation, Dylan gave the Beatles exactly what they were looking for.

Paul McCartney was so intrigued by how he behaved while on weed that he instructed his road manager to write down everything he said, just in case he should decode the secret of the universe in a folk song. About a month later, he had already started pushing his limits, both vocally and instrumentally, on songs such as "She's a Woman," possibly urged by the widened perceptions he gained on pot but no doubt motivated by the desire to capture a piece of Dylan's college-age audience, an older demographic than the teenyboppers that started Beatlemania in the U.S. that February. John Lennon was a little more internally motivated; it was he who was responsible for slipping the muted phrase "turn me on when I get lonely" into the lyrics of "She's a Woman."

Dylan had been similarly changed by the Beatles, for reasons relating more to McCartney's mindset than Lennon's. If marijuana unblocked mental barriers in the Beatles' creative process, Dylan, whose drug-fueled free associations were already running rampant, also gained insights about the real world after his encounter with the group. He'd already assimilated this information soon after hearing "I Want to Hold Your Hand" on a Colorado radio station. Dylan's realizations about the Beatles' success were confirmed when Billboard's April 4, 1964 issue showed the unprecedented occurrence of five Beatles singles occupying all of the top slots on its best selling singles chart as well as eleven of the Top 100, not including the tribute songs "We Love You Beatles" (based on the Conrad Birdie anthem from *Bye Bye Birdie*) by the Caravelles and "A Letter to the Beatles" by the Four Preps. All told, the Beatles placed twenty singles on the Top 100 in 1964 along with six other Lennon and McCartney tunes recorded by Billy J. Kramer and the Dakotas and Cilla Black (who were also managed by Brian Epstein). Although Dylan had been accepted by folk purists, he saw the wider fame and fortune available to him via a singles-buying populace consisting mainly of teenage girls. To Dylan, switching from folk to rock appeared to be an attractive and very doable proposition.

Dylan's latest release, *Another Side of Bob Dylan*, contained several indications of his already waning desire to continue his role as protest music's folk champion, among them "It Ain't Me Babe," "All I Really Want to Do," and the non-protest protest song "Chimes of Freedom." After his confab with the Fab Four in August, Dylan considered the relative lack of commercial success of *Another Side* and moved swiftly toward embracing electric instruments. A sudden leap to rock 'n' roll was not feasible for Dylan, who didn't want to alienate the hip intelligentsia that made up his fan base, but to the diehard folk elitist he began showing a compromise in his style on his next effort, *Bringing It All Back Home*. Beginning in January 1965, Dylan appropriated the updated Chicago blues style of Greenwich Village crony John Hammond Jr., the son of the Columbia Records mogul who first recorded him. Dylan also utilized the sterling session men from Hammond's seminal *So Many Roads* album, including Robbie Robertson, Garth Hudson, and Levon Helm, soon to become members of Dylan's backup group the Band. They were joined by guitarist Michael Bloomfield of the Paul Butterfield Blues Band, who was soon to become infamous as Dylan's whirling dervish electric guitar accomplice at the 1965 Newport Folk Festival.

Dylan's producer Tom Wilson had already begun the conversion process of overdubbing rock arrangements on the previously acoustic *Wednesday Morning, 3 A.M.* by the earnest New York City folkies Simon and Garfunkel. The album juxtaposed folk chestnuts like "You Can Tell the World" alongside the Dylan anthem "The Times They Are A-Changin'" and Paul Simon's early gems "Bleecker Street" and "He Was My Brother," as well as an acoustic version of "The Sounds of Silence." This latter song, when retrofitted with a rock 'n' roll accompaniment a year later, went on to achieve legendary status as a Number One single.

By the end of 1964, the Beatles were adding blues changes and feedback ("I Feel Fine") to their Dylan influence. They were no doubt affected by the burgeoning blues rock scene in England, which included the Animals, the Yardbirds, and the Rolling Stones. Although Paul McCartney added some folk flourishes to "I'll Follow the Sun," the remainder of the Beatles' year was devoted to covers of tunes by their fifties' heroes: Little Richard, Carl Perkins, Buddy Holly, and Chuck Berry.

Berry was also an influence on Dylan, whose 1965 electrified blues rocker "Subterranean Homesick Blues" was based on Berry's "Too Much Monkey Business," from the 1957 LP *After School Session*. (Chuck released *St. Louis to Liverpool*, his second studio album since getting out of jail, in late 1964.)

The song would become Dylan's first Top 40 single as an artist, making its debut on the charts in April 1965. Dylan's famous dead-pan cue card-flipping pantomime of the song, featuring cameo appearances by poet Allen Ginsberg and Dylan's road manager Bob Neuwirth, served as an introduction to D. A. Pennebaker's 1967 documentary *Don't Look Back*, which tracked Dylan's 1965 tour of the UK.

While Dylan was moving inexorably toward rock, the Beatles were back in the studio in February, recording their first all-acoustic number "You've Got to Hide Your Love Away." The song, sung by John Lennon, was the first to show the influence Dylan had on the group. Lennon sang the song in the movie *Help!*, whose soundtrack album, released in August, reached the Top 10 in the U.S. Despite this obvious nod to the folk movement, the *Help!* soundtrack also featured "Ticket to Ride," which Lennon would later proclaim as "the first heavy metal song."

Nevertheless, with the two reigning generals of the incipient rock revolution coming together to exploit the choicest elements of their previously separate creative orientations (to say nothing of the implicit unification of their warring music audiences), the stylistic merger of the Beatles and Bob Dylan brought about a landmark period in rock 'n' roll history, as 1965 became the biggest year for thrilling singles since the arrival of Elvis Presley in 1956.

Every act turned on by either Dylan or the Beatles was forced by the new realities of the marketplace to up their game. The year started with the Beatles' "I Feel Fine" at the top of the charts with "She's a Woman" close behind at Number 5. Phil Spector had achieved a career peak with his production of the Righteous Brothers' "You've Lost That Lovin' Feelin,'" which headed to Number One in February. The Kinks followed up their entry into heavy metal, "You Really Got Me," with "All Day and All of the Night." The Rolling Stones released "Heart of Stone," followed by "The Last Time," with "Play with Fire" as its B side. The Beatles followed up "She's a Woman" with "Ticket to Ride." The Animals followed up their version of John Lee Hooker's "Boom Boom" with "Don't Let Me Be Misunderstood." At the end of February, the Moody Blues arrived with Leiber and Stoller's "Go Now," while the Who made a cameo appearance in March with "I Can't Explain." In April, Bob Dylan officially entered the radio fray with "Subterranean Homesick Blues," followed by his spiritual successors Donovan ("Catch the Wind"), the Byrds ("Mr. Tambourine Man"), and Them with Van Morrison ("Gloria" and "Here Comes the Night"). In June the Rolling Stones delivered their first masterpiece, "Satisfaction." In July came "I Got You Babe" by Sonny & Cher (along with Cher's solo cover of Dylan's "All I Really Want to Do)," "California Girls" by the Beach Boys, "You Were on My Mind" by We Five, "Heart Full of Soul" by the Yardbirds, and Dylan's monumental "Like a Rolling Stone," capping a scintillating month. In August "Help!" arrived, the Turtles covered Dylan's "It Ain't Me Babe," the Animals made an epic out of "We've Gotta Get Out of This Place," Donovan borrowed freely from Dylan in "Colours," Barry McGuire sang P. F. Sloan's desperate "Eve of Destruction," and the Lovin' Spoonful countered with the sprightly "Do You Believe in Magic." In September both Donovan and Glen Campbell covered Buffy Sainte-Marie's anti-war lament "Universal Soldier," while Joan Baez covered protest poet Phil Ochs's "There but for Fortune," and Paul McCartney went totally MOR with "Yesterday."

Bob Dylan was back in October with the rancorous "Positively 4th Street." The Stones returned with the druggy "Get Off My Cloud." During the rest of October, the British group the Silkie claimed one-hit-wonder status with a cover of "You've Got to Hide Your Love Away," the Byrds turned the Pete Seeger prayer "Turn! Turn! Turn!" into a monster hit, and the Yardbirds updated Bo Diddley's "I'm a Man." November gave us the setting for a future Bruce Springsteen oratorio, "It's My Life," by the Animals, "I Can Never Go Home Anymore" by New York City's finest star-crossed girl group, the Shangri-Las, "Don't Think Twice" by the Wonder Who (aka the Four Seasons), "Let's Get Together" (the Dino Valenti-penned anthem in its first single incarnation) by the We Five, the pepped-up arrangement of "The Sounds of Silence" by Simon and Garfunkel, the Hollies' first Top 40 hit "Look Through Any Window," and a new one by the Spoonful, "You Didn't Have to Be So Nice." December was a light month, with only the Kinks' "A

Well Respected Man" and the Beatles' powerful tandem of "We Can Work It Out" and "Day Tripper" fulfilling the needs of rock 'n' roll's rabid new upper demo.

Motown enjoyed a good year in 1965 as well, with the Miracles, Supremes, Temptations, Four Tops, and Marvin Gaye scoring with machine-like efficiency. On his way to perfecting funk, James Brown achieved the first two Top 10 hits of his career with "Papa's Got a Brand New Bag" and "I Got You (I Feel Good)." His prime tormentor Curtis Mayfield wrote his career-defining mellow anthem "People Get Ready" for his group, the Impressions.

As much delight as this sustained run of great singles was producing for the delirious AM radio listening audience, a more essential shift in music business priorities was even then in the wind, led by the unrestrained productivity of the two entities at the top. In March, Dylan's *Bringing It All Back Home* arrived, complete with howling epics like "Gates of Eden," "It's All Over Now, Baby Blue" and the mind-blowing eleven-minute "It's Alright Ma (I'm Only Bleeding)," whose signature line, in which Dylan painted a portrait of a naked President Lyndon Johnson, certainly sang better than it would have looked had MTV been around at the time. The album also contained the full version of "Mr. Tambourine Man" (only one verse had been used by the Byrds in their Number One translation), the fierce Newport '65 opener "Maggie's Farm," and other cryptic gems like "She Belongs to Me," which Rick Nelson (nee Ricky) used to inaugurate his grown-up period in 1969.

Dylan's effort was topped a mere five months later in August with *Highway 61 Revisited*. With this album, the game Dylan had entered just a few short months before was inalterably changed. Michael Bloomfield assumed the lead guitar position later occupied by Robbie Robertson, while Al Kooper (of the Blues Project, by way of the Royal Teens) assumed his perch at the Hammond organ for Dylan's historic recording of "Like a Rolling Stone." This scabrously exhilarating and supremely danceable song simply blew the roof off the established music business. With Dylan singing it at the Newport Folk Festival on the day of its official release, the record alienated whatever remained of Dylan's purist crowd, replacing them with a new nationwide audience of rock hipsters who would now regard albums like works of art and rock stars as poets. (Occasionally, as in the cases of Ed Sanders, owner of the Peace Eye Bookstore, and beat poet/Fugs co-founder Tuli Kupferberg, this worked in reverse.) The album also featured Dylan landmarks of unrestrained hostility and cinematic angst, including "Ballad of a Thin Man," "Just Like Tom Thumb's Blues," "It Takes a Lot to Laugh, It Takes a Train to Cry," and the mind-boggling postcard-from-the-hanging "Desolation Row."

On a two-week tour of North America in August, the Beatles faced a frenzied welter of screaming audiences (New York City, Toronto, Atlanta, Houston, Chicago, Bloomington, Minneapolis, Portland, San Diego, Los Angeles, and San Francisco), all the while watching as "Like a Rolling Stone" became as inescapable in 1965 as "I Want to Hold Your Hand" was in 1964. Inexorably, it moved its way up the charts, from Number 26 to Number 16 to Number 5, finally peaking at Number 2 in the first week of September. Just as chilling were its implications. No longer would the 45 rpm single be the sole measuring stick of rock 'n' roll success. Or even the major one. No longer would screaming teenyboppers be the most desired payoff. The Beatles were becoming a juvenile embarrassment. If they truly wanted to remain competitive (and they did, or at least John and Paul did), they would have to start regarding the 33 1/3 long-playing album as their primary canvas.

In the grip of this creative quantum leap, they started working feverishly on *Rubber Soul* in October, and had it out on the street less than two months later, complete with the double-sided non-album single "We Can Work It Out" backed with "Day Tripper." John's most obvious nod to Dylan was yet to come: "Norwegian Wood," a cryptic ode to sexual revenge and/or getting stoned. *Rubber Soul* also contained John's most heartfelt lyric to date, the autobiographical travelog "In My Life," later covered by the folk world's headmistress Judy Collins. While "The Word" continued the Beatles' long association with what Dylan once described as "just a four-letter word," "Nowhere Man" found John embracing an Age of Aquarius flower-power sensibility, as he pondered an image of his suffering self, exhibiting symptoms of the same disease of irrelevance as the exiled fellow in the jumpsuit eating a peanut butter and banana sandwich who they'd met less than two months before.

Although "We Can Work It Out" was the Beatles fastest selling single since "I Want to Hold Your Hand," their pitched death battle love affair with Bob Dylan was not settled by one mere knockout blow. The two heavyweights were to meet again in New York (1965) and London (April 1966) after Dylan returned from Nashville with the completed *Blonde on Blonde*. By now, the Beatles were starting work on what would become *Revolver*. Hearing Dylan's new UK chart entry "Rainy Day Women #12 and 35," Paul immediately sat down and wrote "Yellow Submarine."

Shortly thereafter, Dylan was filmed with John Lennon in a limo by D. A. Pennebaker. In their brief conversation, the sparring was palpable. As opposed to a folk rock lightweight like Donovan, who Dylan dispensed with a half-hearted jab in *Don't Look Back*, Lennon was an equal, as adept at the empty-eyed put-on as the sardonic master from Minnesota. Had either of them been able to drop their guard, they might have had much to share about fame and its consequences, creativity and its limits, marijuana verses LSD verses alcohol, or abstention. Dylan was still routinely getting booed off stages as a traitor to the cause; the Beatles would soon discover how a slip of the tongue about Jesus could result in a lot of lost business in the American South's Bible Belt. It was in the studio where each found their haven and their respite. In Nashville, studio rates were low. At Abbey Road, they were non-existent.

But sooner or later, reality had to intrude. When faced with gargantuan *Blonde on Blonde* epics like "Sad Eyed Lady of the Lowlands," or even mini-epics like "Visions of Johanna" and "Memphis Blues Again," the cunning "Leopard-skin Pill-box Hat," the perceptive "Just Like a Woman," and the tumultuous "4th Time Around" (a song perhaps pointed at John Lennon), Lennon, for one, had to marvel and laugh. He'd played around with words himself, usually in his books, but this was ridiculous. Lennon and McCartney had their own concerns, no less profound, but expressed them a bit more simply. McCartney painted a portrait of urban loneliness in "Eleanor Rigby" at least as stark and probably a good deal more empathetic than "Visions of Johanna." Harrison's "Taxman" might not have been as subtly cutting as "Leopard-skin Pillbox Hat," but "Doctor Robert" (which was left off the U.S. edition of *Revolver*) was. And with "She Said, She Said," "Tomorrow Never Knows," and "Rain" (the B side of the non-album single "Paperback Writer"), the Beatles proved conclusively that, late to the party or not, no one could write about the drug experience better than they could.

But *Revolver* wouldn't come out in America until August. *Blonde on Blonde* started reaping praise in June. At the same time, on both sides of the Atlantic, competition was rampant. Paul Simon, previously an unknown busker in London, was now being hailed as a folk rock icon with *The Sounds of Silence*, with most of its songs taken from a solo album he'd recorded in England in 1965. *The Paul Simon Song Book* had those tunes in their original form, including "I Am a Rock," "Kathy's Song," "Leaves That Are Green," and "He Was My Brother." The Byrds, Dylan's favorite cover band, came out with *Turn! Turn! Turn!* featuring some of their own Beatlesque material, such as "Set You Free This Time" and "It Won't Be Wrong." Their 1966 singles "Eight Miles High," "5D (Fifth Dimension)," and "Mr. Spaceman" rivaled the Beatles' in charting the unknown regions of inner space. ("She Said, She Said" evolved from a meeting of the two groups, during which they and actor Peter Fonda all sampled LSD.) In New York, the Lovin' Spoonful's John Sebastian did some formidable work whose chief distinguishing feature was its relentlessly upbeat nature. Paul liked "Daydream" enough to base *Revolver*'s "Good Day Sunshine" on its free-floating vibe. In Los Angeles, the Beach Boys, formerly mindless though harmonious devotees of surf music (as the Beatles were devoted followers of R&B and rockabilly), were finding their voice through Brian Wilson. In *Pet Sounds*, released in May, Wilson unveiled a soaring vision of youth's sweet dreams, complicated by drugs and reality, with "God Only Knows," "Wouldn't It Be Nice," "Caroline, No," and especially "I Know There's an Answer" and "I Just Wasn't Made for These Times." Perilously close to his own terrain, McCartney knew, in hearing this album, that the mission of *Revolver* would be to not only top *Pet Sounds*, but to totally blow Wilson out of the water. (At this, he unfortunately succeeded all too well.)

In England more R&B-oriented bands were now using the Beatles' example to start writing more and more of their own material. The Rolling Stones'*Aftermath*, released in April, was their first LP consisting solely of Jagger-Richards compositions, including some nasty tracks like "Mother's Little Helper," "Stupid Girl," and "Under My Thumb." The Yardbirds, now featuring Jeff Beck and Jimmy Page, wrote all their own tracks for *Roger the Engineer*, which was released in the summer. (Only "Over, Under, Sideways, Down" became a hit.) The Who, however, had become a real threat. Led by the ambitious Pete Townshend, their first three singles, "I Can't Explain," "Anyway, Anyhow, Anywhere," and especially "My Generation" were some of the strongest of 1965.

"I wrote the first two songs while I was living in complete squalor, getting stoned every night and listening to Jimmy Reed," Townshend told me. "I was influenced a lot by the Stones. I liked a lot of the Beatles stuff but I was never influenced that much by it. A lot of it was melodic in a way, although it sounded great when they did it; when you tried to find out what it was that made it tick and react to it musically, it was very sort of Italian lovesongs sort of stuff, like 'Yesterday.' How can you be influenced by that?"

Apparently Paul McCartney was listening very carefully to Townshend as the Beatles finished up *Revolver*, and after a desultory tour of America in August, set to work on their next project toward the end of 1966. "The Beatles really liked the mini-opera on *A Quick One*," said Townshend. "Paul McCartney was saying that they were in the recording studio and were doing something similar and that was affecting what they were doing."

By this time, as if living out his own closing lines to onetime soul mate Suze Rotolo in the searing "Ballad in Plain D," Bob Dylan had tested the "chains of the skyway" and found them unforgiving. A July 1966 motorcycle crash in Woodstock took him suddenly and mysteriously out of the running for king of psychedelic free association tone poetry, leaving the field wide open for John Lennon. When he was next heard from outside of Woodstock the world had changed again, due in no small part to the success of the project the Beatles were working on in late 1966 and early 1967: *Sgt. Pepper.*

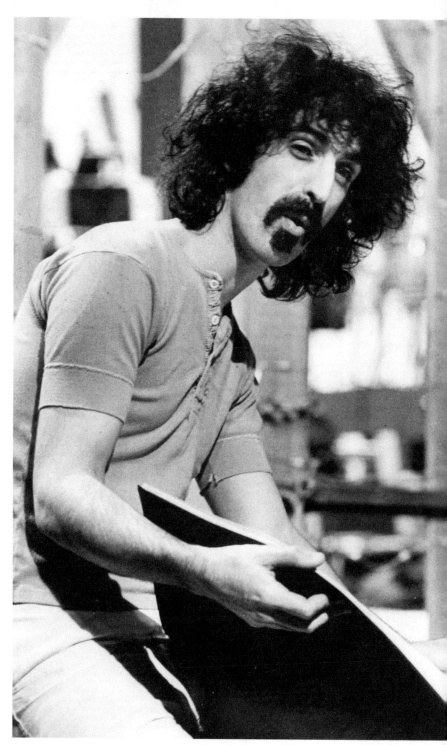

Frank Zappa, circa 1971.

8

ACID ROCK

In some circles, July 29, 1966 is probably thought of as
The Day the Music Died . . . Again.

It is not known whether the Beatles sent any of their emissaries to visit Bob Dylan in the hospital after his motorcycle accident early in August (like Elvis sending his band to visit the laid-up Carl Perkins) or whether Bob Dylan was even in the hospital at all, but the result of Dylan's poor driving skills caused a huge shift in the musical priorities of at least one, if not both of the leading players in the sixties rock revolution. Folk rock took a sharp turn to the right as Dylan emerged at the end of 1967 with the sparse, cryptic *John Wesley Harding*. The pastoral vibes of the Big Pink hideaway in Woodstock, where he recuperated through endless jam sessions with the Band, turned into *The Basement Tapes* and effectively took the air out of his prose balloon, deflating the entire scene and its attendant megalomaniacal prophesies in the bargain. With records by the Byrds, Gram Parsons, and the Band's first solo album, country rock espoused a back-to-Big-Pink ethos far removed from the street-fighting politics that dominated the fall of Aquarius.

The Beatles had their own problems, which they attempted to patch up with a press conference in Chicago preceding their first American concert of 1966, in which John Lennon tearfully proclaimed that neither he nor the rest of the band was bigger than Jesus. Nobody believed him, but it didn't matter. Once they completed the last date of the tour in San Francisco, they announced they were done with touring forever. From now on Abbey Road would be their Big Pink, where they could noodle around to their heart's content (and on EMI's dime).

In 1966 San Francisco folk rock merged with LSD to form acid rock. A heady mixture of rock, folk, blues, and self indulgence, the genre seemed, at times, to be a test of the limits an audience could be induced to listen to Jerry Garcia's guitar solos. As it turned out, these limits were virtually unlimited. Garcia and his former jug band were now the Grateful Dead, a kind of house band for Ken Kesey's Merry Pranksters and their Trips Festivals, mind-expanding environmental art showcases where LSD was freely available. One of the side benefits of LSD, it turned out, was the ability to not only tolerate, but to get deeply into extended guitar solos, whether perpetrated by Garcia or any of the dozens of B. B. King-influenced players around town, in bands called Big Brother and the Holding Company, the Jefferson Airplane, the Steve Miller Band, Mother Earth, Moby Grape, and Country Joe and the Fish. In 1966, largely because of these bands, San Francisco was not only attracting every disaffected young pot smoker on the conti-nent, hoping to find free love on Haight Street, but also every ju-nior A&R man with a checkbook.

On one of his independent visits to San Francisco in 1967, Paul took note of Kesey's Day-Glo painted bus, in which the Merry Pranksters traveled from place to place spreading their anarchic message of "turn on, tune in, drop out" as preached by Dr. Timo-thy Leary, the radical Stanford professor, and decided to create the film *Magical Mystery Tour*. By then the Beatles were well into this phi-losophy, although as practiced by McCartney (who did not admit to taking LSD until 1967), dropping out didn't involve giving up music. In fact, by turning on and tuning in, he was producing some of his greatest stuff ever, as evidenced by the just completed *Sgt. Pepper's Lonely Hearts Club Band*, which he was quick to impress upon Brian Wilson, whose home he visited in Los Angeles, playing him a snatch of "She's Leaving Home." Wilson, whose *Pet Sounds* had inspired McCartney, was working on *Smile* at the time, a potential magnum opus of Gershwinesque epics like "Surf's Up" and "Cab-inessence" along with quirky gems like "Vegetables" that might have kept him in the same breath as the Beatles. But the pressure was too much. He never finished his dream album, releasing instead the tepid *Smiley Smile* around the same time as *Sgt. Pepper*, with only "Heroes and Villains" and "Good Vibrations" to redeem it.

In Los Angeles, Frank Zappa, leader of the symphonic and satirical Mothers of Invention, generally dismissed the San Francisco scene as so much high school posturing, preferring Edgar Varese to B. B. King. He also preferred L.A.'s authenticity, of the sort that could only be found in the exclusive Laurel Canyon neighborhood where Joni Mitchell was shacked up with David Crosby and/or Graham Nash, Carole King was jamming with James Taylor, and everyone famous lived in a house once owned by someone even more famous. (The house where Zappa lived with his wife and guests such as the GTOs, Alice Cooper, and various other freeloaders and sidemen, and where he created the Mothers' debut double album *Freak Out*, had previously belonged to cowboy star Tom Mix, whose horse was reportedly buried beneath the basement.)

Furthering the mystical drift of the times and the Beatles' music, George Harrison spent the first few weeks after the 1966 tour ended in India on sabbatical, taking a master class with renowned sitar player Ravi Shankar, whose music he was introduced to in 1965 by the Byrds' Roger McGuinn. Intrigued by the sitar ever since playing around with one on the set of *Help!* George had used it on several tunes: "Norwegian Wood," "Love You To," and "Tomorrow Never Knows." Upon returning to London, George was eager to insinuate its droning presence into a new song. It wasn't just the droning presence of the sitar, but the droning Indian philosophy that he'd been absorbing as well. This opportunity would come up in March 1967, three months into the recording of *Sgt. Pepper*, when Harrison invited members of the Asian Music Center to join him in the studio to play indigenous Indian instruments like the dilruba, swarmandal, tambura, and tabla on "Within You, Without You," about as cogent a recap of his current anti-materialist mode of thinking as he'd yet written.

By then, John and Paul were deeply into what Paul had already earmarked as their version of *Freak Out*, Frank Zappa's multi-leveled, often cacophonous statement of life in Los Angeles. Released in June 1966, *Freak Out* came complete with riot police, unrestrained paranoia, random snatches of street corner doo-wop, the occasional audience-baiting snarl, and two mind-blowing re-creations of an acid trip (or at least songs that made much more sense if you were on acid), "Help, I'm a Rock" and "The Return of the Son of Monster Magnet." Naturally, Paul's vision for what turned out to be *Sgt. Pepper* was a bit more muted, whimsical, and nostalgic, originally devised as a kind of sentimental return to the Beatles' respective childhood haunts, with "Penny Lane" and "Strawberry Fields Forever" two of the first three tracks of the concept completed (the first was "When I'm Sixty-Four."). Although these were great tracks, they were a far cry from a freak out, which even Paul realized when he summoned the group into a session following the completion of "Penny Lane." As a favor to a friend in the avant-garde circles in which he was then running (courtesy of girlfriend Jane Asher's brother Peter), Paul had agreed to contribute a piece to a "happening" called "The Carnival of Light." The ensuing fourteen-minute mash of mumbles, screams, odd notes, and echoes was claimed by Paul to be his answer to the experimental music of Karlheinz Stockhausen or John Cage. But a thumb in the eye of Frank Zappa seems more likely to have been the case.

This was all rendered moot by a contractual anomaly of the British music business, whereby when "Penny Lane" and "Strawberry Fields Forever" were first released as singles, their use on the album in progress was precluded, scotching the nostalgia premise from the get-go. ☞

Whatever the Beatles' original plans were for the sequencing of *Sgt. Pepper,* these were rendered moot by a development in the communications business in America, leading late in 1966 to the opening up of the FM band on the radio dial, previously a province of dead air and classical music. Banned from duplicating the programming of their AM equivalents, radio station owners were forced to somehow fill the time. Into this breach rode the intrepid record companies with their newly-signed roster of bands that were under the influence of

Dylan, the Beatles, and LSD (not necessarily in that order), bands that were just then disdaining the outmoded three-minute single in favor of the nine-minute tone poem or the five-minute guitar solo (often in the same song). By early 1967 "free form" FM radio had popped up in college towns across the country, commandeering larger markets like New York (WOR and WNEW), San Francisco (KMPX), and Los Angeles (KMET). *Sgt. Pepper*'s release in June 1967 came just in time to serve as the unofficial soundtrack for what the San Francisco Chamber of Commerce proclaimed was "The Summer of Love," with enough free-form FM outlets in place to blast the soundtrack nationwide (three times in a row in its entirety if the DJ felt like it). AM stations generally stuck with the 1967 singles "Penny Lane" / "Strawberry Fields Forever," "All You Need Is Love" / "Baby You're a Rich Man," and "Hello Goodbye" / "I Am the Walrus," all of which appeared on the *Magical Mystery Tour* soundtrack album, although FM jocks and fans could have experienced *Sgt. Pepper* as it was originally intended had any of them been privy to McCartney's abandoned plans.

In the meantime, as George had gone to India as if in preparation for the masterpiece-in-waiting, John Lennon experienced his own life-changing epiphany. On November 9, 1966, he was attending the opening of an art exhibit at the Indica Gallery in London titled *Unfinished Paintings and Objects* when he met the woman who was to eventually influence the remainder of his career and life: Yoko Ono.

Unlike George and his studies of Indian philosophy and the sitar, Yoko had little or no impact on *Sgt. Pepper*. At first she saw John merely as a potential buyer of her unfinished paintings and objects. But pretty soon she would insinuate herself into his life, influencing the rest of his Beatles output in a manner far more openly and completely than George's Indian instruments or philosophy ever could. For a while it was neck and neck as to who would have the greater sway over the remainder of the Beatles' time as a functioning rock band.

For most fans, to even contemplate the notion of a music scene without the Beatles in it was a prospect more depressing than dealing with the absent Dylan, who spent the rest of 1966 and all of 1967 on the sidelines. In the meantime, marijuana had become passé in the face of the psychic challenges offered by LSD, resulting in the decline of the brainy if undanceable folk rock in favor of the all-day, all-over, out-of-body experience of psychedelia, personified by Jerry Garcia's smile, Jimi Hendrix's use of the phasing effect (borrowed from the Beatles' "Tomorrow Never Knows"), and the warped poetry of Lewis Carroll. Carroll had become a cult figure among San Francisco hippies after the Jefferson Airplane immortalized his children's book *Alice in Wonderland* with their Top 10 hit "White Rabbit." About this time, the Incredible String Band, a particular favorite of John's, recorded "The Mad Hatter's Song" for their second album, the hugely influential *The 5000 Spirits or the Layers of the Onion*, a Middle Eastern-sounding opus that also included "Chinese White," "The Hedgehog's Song," "My Name Is Death," and the haunting "First Girl I Loved." Second to none in his devotion to Carroll (and LSD), John set to work on "I Am the Walrus" in September 1967, the title inspired by the Carroll poem *The Walrus and the Carpenter*. Still mourning the recent death of Beatles manager Brian Epstein and seething about what Dylan had been able to "get away with" during his prime, Lennon was in rare bilious form, exorcising and entertaining his demons while prodding George Martin to reach new heights in the art of production. It was about as close to madness as a single was apt to get (apart from Napoleon XIV's 1966 hit "They're Coming to Take Me Away, Ha-Haa!" which was all about insanity).

Had John ventured any closer to the abyss, he might have followed in the path of the unfortunate Syd Barrett, founder of Pink Floyd, and author of their first two singles, "Arnold Layne" and the follow up, "See Emily Play," a big UK hit in the summer of 1967. Recording their first album *Piper at the Gates of Dawn* at Abbey Road under the auspices of former Beatles engineer Norman Smith, Pink Floyd used a lot of the studio tricks that the Beatles pioneered. They were introduced to the Beatles while *Sgt. Pepper* was being completed. Not much was said, but a couple of weeks later, on April 29, Pink Floyd was the headline attraction at a major psychedelic event of music, drugs, and poetry at the Alexandra Palace called "The 14-Hour Technicolour Dream," which also featured Savoy Brown, the Pretty Things, the Soft Machine, and the Crazy World of Arthur Brown. Pink Floyd apparently took the stage at just about the fourteenth hour, or sometime in the early morning of the following day. LSD had been declared illegal, so many audience members were stoned on STP, a new and much stronger variant. One attendee was Syd Barrett, whose lead guitar playing that morning was particularly inspired on tunes like "Astronomy Domine" and "Interstellar Overdrive." If Pink Floyd was anointed at that event as heirs to the psychedelic future, it may have been one of the last great performances their lead guitarist and main songwriter would ever give. For much of the next year, until he was formally kicked out of the band, his mind and life would be dominated by hallucinogens, leading to his eventual hospitalization and an early retirement.

The ever-competitive Lennon was there to witness the festivities, also in a similar state of risk, as evidenced by his recent spaced-out trilogy of psychedelic gems: "Strawberry Fields Forever," "A Day in the Life," and "Lucy in the Sky with Diamonds." Five months later, "I Am the Walrus" continued the trend, making it painfully clear that none of the other Beatles had enough influence over the headstrong Lennon to stop him, even if they had wanted to do so.

Also on the bill that night was multi-media artist Yoko Ono, whose contribution, called "Cut Piece," was modeled on some of her earlier groundbreaking performances. Audience members were summoned to the stage, handed a pair of scissors, and instructed to snip the clothes off a model perched on a stepladder. (On other occasions, Yoko generously sacrificed her own wardrobe for her art.) Attending the concert with John and Paul was John Dunbar, owner of the Indica Gallery, who'd hosted the exhibit where John first met Yoko, which would have given John easy access to her that night. But apparently the two gentlemen, suffering from a bit of psychedelic claustrophobia, slipped out for a smoke and the meeting didn't happen. But it was just another example, beyond music, beyond drugs, of Yoko's karmic inevitability.

Meanwhile, free from the rigors of touring and the admonishments of Brian Epstein, the Beatles lounged in the studio, working on *Magical Mystery Tour*, an album and television film devised by McCartney mainly to give the band something to do in the wake of Epstein's passing. Early in the process, a recent signing in the EMI stable caught their fancy: the Bonzo Dog Doo-Dah Band. Previously, George Martin had produced the trad jazz group the New Temperance Seven. In addition to playing parodies of their music, Bonzo wits Neil Innes and Viv Stanshall indulged in Frank Zappian satire. They were quickly enlisted to play a song from their first album *Gorilla* in *Magical Mystery Tour*, the Presleyesque "Death Cab for Cutie," which would become the name of a popular indie band some thirty years later. In 1968 Paul McCartney co-produced "I'm the Urban Spaceman," a Top five UK hit from the album *The Doughnut in Granny's Greenhouse* (named for the U.S. hit single), which also contained "We Are Normal," "Can a Blue Man Sing the Whites," and "Trouser Press," the latter becoming the name of a popular indie music magazine five years later. Innes would eventually ally himself with the Monty Python comedy troupe and then joined Paul McCartney's brother Mike in the band Grimms before arriving at his ultimate destiny as a Beatle parodist in the Rutles along with Pythonite Eric Idle. Their crowning achievement was a 1976 *Saturday Night Live* skit that was turned into a full-fledged TV movie in 1978 called *All You Need Is Cash*, a fab faux documentary complete with Beatlesque soundtrack album. Although George and John were big fans of the parodies, Paul McCartney was lukewarm at best. ATV Music, the Beatles' then-publisher, was also not amused, suing Innes for copyright infringement. The fact that the settlement put the Lennon-McCartney brand alongside Innes's on songs like "Ouch!" "Piggy in the Middle," "Cheese and Onions," and "Hold My Hand" is a satirical statement in itself.

The Beatles had already been roundly spoofed by Zappa in the Mothers of Invention's third album *We're Only in It for the Money*, released in the spring of 1968, which contained such all-purpose anti-Summer of Love sentiments as "Who Needs the Peace Corps?" "Flower Punk," and "Concentration Moon."

By then the Beatles were safely ensconced in the protective aura of the Maharishi Mahesh Yogi in Rishikesh, India, where they learned how to meditate and wean themselves off LSD (but not marijuana). Ringo left the compound after ten days due to his food allergies. Paul left a short time later, perhaps in a last ditch attempt to save his relationship with Jane Asher. (He failed.) George and John stayed the longest, decamping only after being convinced by a member of their entourage that the Maharishi had been making improper sexual advances to one of the women campers. During their stay, the Beatles were uncommonly productive, stockpiling dozens of songs that would fill out their remaining three albums, including John's "Sexy Sadie," a fierce indictment of the humbled guru.

If Lennon was miffed about leaving, George Harrison was still pretty mellow, having spent January in Bombay, where he scored the film *Wonderwall*, a voyeuristic tale in which French singer Jane Birkin played a character named Penny Lane. Out of this experience came the basis for one of his best songs, "The Inner Light," recorded just before returning to India to huddle with the Maharishi. George's score to *Wonderwall* would be the first release on the Beatles' new boutique record label, Apple.

But the good vibes didn't last more than a month. It was then that John Lennon, obviously back on LSD, spoke to the Apple executive board for the first time, amending his August 1966 announcement in Chicago by stating that he alone was Jesus Christ. Nobody dared contradict him. A day later, with his wife Cynthia out of town, John finally consummated his relationship with Yoko, but not before recording an entire album of semi-atmospheric trance music with her titled *Unfinished Music No. 1: Two Virgins*. Two weeks later, when sessions started on what was to become "The White Album" at the end of May, the bad vibes got ugly when John violated the sanctuary of the studio by bringing Yoko along. Even worse, he insisted on making his political views the subject of the Beatles next single, the waffling "Revolution." Ostensibly a "make-love-not-war" treatise, "Revolution" was not meant to be part of the countercultural drift into violence that marked 1968 and 1969.

In its first rendition, which ended up on "The White Album," Lennon seemed to want it both ways, counting himself both "out" and "in" such a revolution. At that contentious first session, the song devolved into an extended jam, which John (and the by now indispensible Yoko) turned into a semi-atmospheric bit of uneasy listening they called "Revolution 9," John's answer to Paul's answer to Frank Zappa's experimental music. Later, John re-recorded an up-tempo version that was used on the B side of "Hey Jude." In this version, he revealed his true feelings (he wanted "out"). He would later make his way back into the middle of things, but the Beatles would be all but broken up by then.

After this inauspicious start, the sojourn to Rishikesh took on even more significance, as the individual Beatles had plenty of material at their disposal to work on, rather than having to count on their usual studio chemistry to provide inspiration. This cosmic windfall proved to be a good thing, given that Paul was breaking up with Jane and hooking up with Linda Eastman, John was shacking up with Yoko while divorcing Cynthia, and George was becoming infatuated with a new love, the Moog synthesizer, which he used to promising effect on "Here Comes the Sun," "Because," and his 1969 solo album *Electronic Sound*, released in May, 1969.

In the end, if it was love that undid them, it was not the kind they usually sang about; it was John's obsessive love for drugs, sex, and Yoko, and Paul's for control, work, and the Beatles.

Under Yoko's influence, John's final contribution to "The White Album" was the poignant love song to his mother "Julia," a symbolic passing of the torch to his new muse. The album, simply titled *The Beatles*, was released in October 1968, a month before the election of Richard M. Nixon effectively signaled the beginning of the end of the countercultural revolution that John Lennon would belatedly join. The remainder of the decade would find him tethered to Yoko in various experiments in art, political theater, and questionable (if undeniably personal) music: *Unfinished Music No. 1: Two Virgins* (November 1968), *Unfinished Music No. 2: Life with the Lions* (May 1969), and *Wedding Album* (November 1969). One month later, the Plastic Ono Band's *Live Peace in Toronto 1969* came out, featuring "Give Peace a Chance," "Cold Turkey" (John's admission of his heroin addiction), and Yoko's inimitable "Don't Worry Kyoko (Mummy's Only Looking for Her Hand in the Snow)."

While preparing individual solo albums in January 1969, the other Beatles attempted and failed to record another album (*Let It Be*), filmed a rooftop concert (which was interrupted by the police), brought in the shady and divisive Allen Klein to handle their business affairs (over Paul's objections), and in February, finally started the more fruitful sessions that would result in *Abbey Road*. In March, John and Paul married their new paramours. John and Yoko started using heroin in June and got into a car accident in July. Yoko then brought a bed into the studio for the rest of the deteriorating *Abbey Road* sessions, which wouldn't wrap until August.

Outside the doors of Abbey Road, the competition was heating up. At the end of 1968 the Rolling Stones issued the highly regarded *Beggar's Banquet*. In December 1969 they would follow it up with the unfortunately titled *Let It Bleed*, which seemed like a Mick Jagger joke aimed at the Beatles' abandoned *Let It Be* album (Jagger denied it). A day after the album's release, the humor turned grisly when the Stones presided over the Hell's Angels stabbing death of a member of the audience at the Altamont Speedway Free Festival. Forbidding tracks like "Gimme Shelter" and "Midnight Rambler" aptly summed up the blood-soaked year of the album's inception, which also included the Charles Manson killing spree in the Hollywood Hills. (The scenario unfortunately involved several Beatles songs, most famously "Helter Skelter," the Beatles' attempt to outdo Pete Townshend's thunderous rock sound with the Who.)

Townshend, whose mini-opera "A Quick One While He's Away" influenced Paul McCartney during the sessions for *Sgt. Pepper*, had moved forcefully into maxi-opera mode, creating *Tommy* in May 1969. As the hit "Pinball Wizard" raced up the British Top 10, McCartney was perhaps inspired to create the famous medley that dominated Side 2 of *Abbey Road*. Townshend and McCartney, however, never admitted to being influenced by each other. Instead, they credited a pair of 1967 singles by Keith Hopkins (aka Keith West), the relatively obscure "Excerpt from a Teenage Opera (Grocer Jack)" and its follow up "Sam," both coming from an unproduced rock opera. West went on to join the psychedelic band Tomorrow, which released its only eponymous album in 1968.

In defiance of the year's prevailing foul mood, Bob Dylan continued his drift from the imposed requirements of his audience by perpetrating an innocuous country album, *Nashville Skyline*, which was released in April 1969. Despite the close proximity of his home to the Woodstock Music and Art Fair, which took place in August, Dylan left town well before the hordes descended. Unlike Lennon, he realized that the moment for such flowery sentiments had long since passed. As if to confirm this theory, Elvis Presley, playing on the momentum of his 1968 TV special, triumphantly returned to Las Vegas at the end of August. "Suspicious Minds," his first Number One single since 1962, was released in September, the same month *Abbey Road* came out. Once again, the two ships were moving in opposite directions, in a reversal of their positions when they first met in 1965.

In 1970 John Lennon recorded "Instant Karma" with his old idol, irascible producer Phil Spector. So impressed was John by Spector's quick turnaround that he immediately invited him to salvage the previously abandoned *Let It Be* project. Spector, who was at loose ends since playing a drug dealer in *Easy Rider*, was more than happy to tackle the job. His arrangement of "The Long and Winding Road," done without Paul's knowledge or approval, proved to be the final indignity. Although the Beatles had unofficially broken up after finishing *Abbey Road*, Paul made it official after hearing Spector's work.

Let It Be was released in May 1970, with "The Long and Winding Road" ironically serving as the band's twentieth and last American Number One hit. One month later, *Self Portrait*, Dylan's half-assed pastiche of assorted covers and live performances was released. It was one of the worst-reviewed albums of his career (and deservedly so), and seemed to signal the end of his career as well. But Dylan would have the last laugh in 1975, when the first of several artistic and commercial comebacks occurred with the release of *Blood on the Tracks*, followed in short order by the official release of

The Basement Tapes and 1976's *Desire*. The rest of the 1970s would provide him with four more hit albums. By this time, Elvis Presley was dead and buried and the Beatles were no more than a memory of collective brilliance marred by their all too human individual achievements.

The Byrds.

9

THE AMERICAN BEATLES

So alarming and unprecedented was the Beatles' 1964
takeover of the American Top 40 singles chart that it took a moment for the arbiters of culture to adjust to it. But their output was so perfectly pitched to the moment, artistically polished, and prolific that it was difficult if not impossible to find any American rock band capable of copying it. At first, all radio programmers and their hungry audiences could do was let in a slew of the Beatles' Merseybeat brethren to handle the overflow, including Gerry and the Pacemakers, the Dave Clark Five, Herman's Hermits, the Seekers, and Billy J. Kramer and the Dakotas, not to mention the Rolling Stones, the Kinks, the Yardbirds, and the Who.

Prior to the Beatles' arrival on the U.S. charts in 1964, the sound of a real live rock band on Top 40 radio or anywhere else was a rare commodity. Only in 1959 did rock bands make any sort of a dent, but these were instrumental groups such as Johnny and the Hurricanes, the Wailers, the Fireballs, Rock-a-Teens, the Virtues, the Megatrons, the Wild-Cats, and the Frantics. In 1961, Paul Revere and the Raiders came on like another instrumental group with "Like Long Hair."

From the end of 1961 through 1963, New York City's Joey Dee and the Starliters had nothing else on their mind but extolling the virtues of the twist. On the other coast, the surf craze began in late 1961, popularized by guitarist Dick Dale ("Let's Go Trippin'") and the Beach Boys ("Surfin'"). This was also primarily an instrumental genre, with groups like the Surfaris, the Marketts, the Pyramids, and the Rivingtons offering very little in the way of lyric substance. The Rivingtons' "Papa-Oom-Mow-Mow" (1962) was a virtual doo-wop send up. The lyrics to "Wipe Out" by the Surfaris (1963) consisted of the title phrase maniacally cackled by the group's manager. Similarly single-minded, the Beach Boys followed up "Surfin" with "Surfin' Safari," "Surfin' U.S.A.," and "Surfer Girl," which took them to the end of 1963, at which point Brian Wilson began to emerge with "Be True to Your School" and the lonely, wounded "In My Room." This introspective phase didn't last, however, as "Fun, Fun, Fun," "I Get Around," and "Dance, Dance, Dance" dominated 1964, interrupted only by the plaintive "When I Grow Up (To Be a Man)" and the contemplative B side "Don't Worry Baby." By this time, surf music (and its complementary sidetrack, hot rod music) had invaded inland ports as various as Minneapolis, Minnesota ("Surfin' Bird" by the Trashmen), Nashville, Tennessee ("G.T.O." by Ronny and the Daytonas), South Bend, Indiana ("California Sun" by the Rivieras) and Boulder, Colorado ("Baja" by the Astronauts).

Aside from the fluke success of "Louie Louie" by the Kingsmen in 1963, vocal groups prevailed, including a second wave of post-doo-wop, Italian white soul acts, including Randy and the Rainbows, the Duprees, the Belmonts (sans Dion, who was now accompanied by the Del Satins), the Excellents, Vito and the Salutations, the Capris, and the Four Seasons. In addition, girl-group sounds were waiting in the wings by the Ronettes, the Shirelles, the Chantels, the Angels, the Exciters, the Jaynetts, and the Shangri-Las. Motown was already happening with its stable of lite R&B, with an occasional genius track by Smokey Robinson, the Temptations, the Four Tops, or Marvin Gaye thrown in. The teen idols of Dick Clark's *American Bandstand*, including Frankie Avalon, Bobby Rydell, Freddy Cannon, and Fabian were holding on to their 1950s moments. The big news at the time was the folk music revival, brought on by the enlightened politics of J.F.K., with Peter, Paul and Mary (covering Dylan), the New Christy Minstrels (covering Pete Seeger), the Chad Mitchell Trio (with future Byrds founder McGuinn backing them up on guitar), and the Big Three (with Cass Elliot, later of the Mamas and the Papas), plus holdovers from the previous folk music revival: the Kingston Trio, the Brothers Four, and the Highwaymen.

In the entire history of rock 'n' roll to that point, going back to its rockabilly beginnings circa 1956, only the Crickets could qualify as a self-contained four-man unit, led by a brilliant songwriter (Buddy Holly) and his in-house backup band. Admittedly, Gene Vincent had his Blue Caps, and Elvis had D. J., Scotty, and Bill, but those guys weren't looked upon as co-equals with the lead singer; they were studio assemblages, touring necessities. Even the Crickets evolved into Buddy Holly and the Crickets (to some extent for contractual reasons, but also because that was the tradition; even the Rock 'n Roll Trio morphed into Johnny Burnette and the Rock 'n Roll Trio). In any case, Gene Vincent hadn't had a hit since 1957, Buddy Holly had been gone since 1959, and Elvis Presley was leaning more toward moviemaking than rock, mired in a fourteen- song losing streak without a Number One record. (During 1962 and 1963 he completed movies nine through fourteen.) American kids were too busy doing the twist and watching themselves being celebrated doing the twist to worry about picking up an instrument or writing a song.

Into this void stepped the Beatles, who were first of all from England, where Gene Vincent had settled in 1963; where Buddy Holly and the Crickets had had five Top 20 hits since 1960; and where five of the Everly Brothers' ten U.S. flops in 1962 and 1963 made the UK Top 40. The Beatles had been raised on Gene, Buddy, Don and Phil, and Elvis; they devoured every obscure R&B B side they could find in Brian Epstein's record store. They were enamored of Motown. They dug Arthur Alexander. They virtually cloned the Brill Building's two-minute hit formula. Plus, they had their own look: a little bit preppy and a little bit scruffy. In fact, they were a little bit too good for rock 'n' roll, but not so arch as the cardigan-clad folk singers. They were bright, witty, and possessed an undeniable chemistry. When they shook their shaggy heads in unison, they became the first headbangers. And there were four of them. For girls that meant four separate love objects. For guys that meant four separate rock 'n' role identities to choose from.

Soon after the Beatles' first appearance on *The Ed Sullivan Show* in February 1964, Roger McGuinn (then known as Jim), was walking down a street in Greenwich Village, his hair creeping out past his collar, carrying an electric guitar. As he walked, he could hear club owners whispering to each other as he passed by, "What we need is four of him."

With so few rock bands to choose from, a bunch had to be created pretty much on the spot. Luckily, the Beatles' TV appearance prodded a significant number of wide-eyed kids to pick up electric guitars, and an even more significant number of somber solo folkies to abandon their principles and go for the gusto and the gold in groups. By 1965, McGuinn and his new group were at the top of the chart with Dylan's "Mr. Tambourine Man," and these same taste makers were calling the Byrds "The American Beatles."

But this was not entirely accurate. There could never be an American Beatles, certainly not after 1964. The Beatles had done too many things too perfectly, nailing the time and the place, the energy and the magic, and the look and the sound to allow for such a happenstance. The Byrds did have some nice Beatlesque harmonies and a decent songwriting bent, but they were much more allied with Dylan and the nascent folk rock sound, which the Beatles dabbled in but certainly not exclusively. The problem and the beauty of the Beatles was that they dabbled in everything and the only thing they treasured was a good song, of which they wrote many more than they knew what to do with. ☞

The Beatles wrote so many good songs that within a year or two they changed the shape of the Top 40, to say nothing of the record and radio business. Prior to their arrival, dating back to 1957, the number of singles entered onto the Top 100 went steadily up, from 483 in 1957 to 681 in 1961. During the heyday of the twist, the numbers dwindled a bit, but in 1964, the year of the Beatles arrival, 714 singles made the Top 100, an almost ten per cent increase over the previous year. The numbers soared in the next two years, peaking at an all-time high of 743 in 1966. There was then a steady decline until 1974, when only 492 singles made the charts, a level not seen since 1957. This phenomenon can be partly credited to the Beatles' shift in 1967 to *Sgt. Pepper* mode, as the album became a work of art and the single was reduced to an afterthought. This attitude, like most of the Beatles' attitudes, quickly permeated the thinking of the rest of the American music community as well as the record labels, who were now more concerned with the album chart rather than the singles chart.

If there could never be any one American Beatles, at least their sound could be broken up into more easily clonable pieces and dispersed to the clamoring throngs of Beatle-inspired bands that started showing up for record company auditions as early as 1965, ready to take their place on the radio in 1966. And thus, seven new rock group-oriented Top 40 styles evolved to co-exist with the recently-minted folk rock of 1965: sunshine pop, garage rock (the high school dropout's answer to 1965's frat rock), acid rock, psychedelic pop, psychedelic rock, baroque rock, and power pop. Many of these labels were fluid, with the same bands and songs being identified for each one. Many of the bands disowned such labels as soon as they found out about them. They were only playing what was in their hearts or (sadly) issuing what the record company told them was the hit. And from 1965 through the end of the sixties and into the seventies they produced something that sounded like the Beatles. This might have frustrated if not broken up a lot of young bands, but nevertheless, it provided an amazing amount of enjoyment to connoisseurs of the 45 in its waning heyday.

One of the next bands to be dubbed with the American Beatles jinx was the Remains, a group from Boston that was more like a garage band version of the Rolling Stones. Although they signed with Epic Records and once toured with the Beatles in 1966, Barry Tashian's band never had a charting single or album, despite being championed by influential rock critic Jon Landau. Their first and last singles, "Why Do I Cry" and "Don't Look Back," were collected on the garage band compendium *Nuggets: Original Artyfacts from the First Psychedelic Era*, curated by noted rock 'n' roll geek and Patti Smith guitarist Lenny Kaye.

Openly coveting the same jinx was the Monkees, a blatantly contrived media takeover designed to capture the least discriminating portion of the Beatles' audience. The Monkees owed a debt to the format of the 1950s TV show *The Adventures of Ozzie and Harriet*, in which teen idol Ricky Nelson entertained the masses with a new song every week. It also drew inspiration from the Beatles' own *A Hard Day's Night*, which featured the lads romping through the strawberry fields of superstardom without raising a sweat. The Monkees were Don Kirshner's cash cow, a way to capture the image without all the hard work, and secondarily, to give his stable of former Brill Building songwriters (now relocated to L.A.) an easy outlet for their material.

Ironically, the Monkees' records succeeded far better than their TV show. The exceptionally well-crafted hit "Last Train to Clarksville" was provided by staff songwriter-producers Tommy Boyce and Bobby Hart, kicking off the concept in high style in September 1966. This was followed in December by Neil Diamond's "I'm a Believer" and "A Little Bit Me, a Little Bit You" the following March, Goffin and King's "Pleasant Valley Sunday" in July, Kingston Trio stand-in John Stewart's "Daydream Believer" in November, and Boyce and Hart's "Valleri," their last Top 10 hit, in March 1968. (The latter featured one of the all-time great Top 40 guitar parts, played by studio ace Louie Shelton.) Boyce and Hart produced and wrote most of the tunes for the group's first album, *The Monkees*, which spent an amazing thirteen weeks at Number One, displacing *Revolver*. Since *Sgt. Pepper* wouldn't arrive for another nine months, this gave the team plenty of time to release *More of the Monkees*, which came out in February 1967 and sat at the top spot for eighteen weeks. Their third album *Headquarters* spent only one week at the top before *Sgt. Pepper* arrived to restore order to the universe. But after *Sgt. Pepper* peaked, the Monkees returned to the top spot with *Pisces, Aquarius, Capricorn & Jones, Ltd*, remaining there until the end of 1967. In 1968 the show was cancelled and so were the Monkees, but not before giving the world the epic psychedelic movie *Head*, which critic Pauline Kael called "some potsmoker's dream," a fact that by itself should have guaranteed the Monkees a decent post-TV career.

The only thing wrong with this equation was that the Monkees weren't really a rock band, or any kind of band at all. Or were they?

"I've heard that Mick said later that we weren't the Monkees any more than Lorne Greene was a Cartwright," their bass player Peter Tork told me. "At the same time, we *were* the Monkees. It was a unique phenomenon, to be a member of a group that wasn't a group and yet was a group. If we'd been a group, we would have fought to be a group, or we would have broken up as a group. But we were a project, a TV show, a record-making machine. Being a member of a synthetic group, I suffered from the criticisms— those no talent schmucks from the street—while in the meantime, I wasn't able to make the music I thought needed to be made. From the producers you'd run into a lot of 'You guys are not the Lovin' Spoonful, so shut up.'"

If Mick Dolenz and Davy Jones left a lot to be desired musically, Peter Tork and Mike Nesmith were proven folk musicians. Like Dylan, Tork left college in Minnesota to play the basket houses of Greenwich Village before beating out Stephen Stills for the TV role of a lifetime. "When the Monkees made their pilot," he said, "the four of us got on stage and we were supposed to be doing a dance set. Mike had his guitar. I had my bass. Mick knew two beats on the drums. During breaks in the filming we asked the stage crew to fire up the amps and, never having played together before on the same stage, we knocked out a song and the audience liked us. Some people from Capitol Records who heard us said they would have signed us even if we hadn't had the TV show."

If true, this would have been either a testament to the Monkees' native ability, or an example of the desperation sweeping the music business in 1966, even at the Beatles' own label, to keep up with the demand for product. Once signed, however, recording presented its own challenges. "Davy played nothing but tambourine," said Tork, "so he had his part down after the second take. Mickey never did believe he was a decent drummer. Mike wanted to produce his own records. He wanted total control. I was the only one who believed in the group per se, and so there I was, all by myself, wanting a group, with nobody to be a group with."

Part of the evolution/revolution wrought by the Beatles was the opportunity they created for rock and pop rock bands to not only co-exist but to dominate the industry. This may have resulted in some great music being heard on the radio, but most of these bands had never paid their dues in an established underground setting, like the Beatles did in Hamburg. They also rarely had devoted management and a sympathetic producer, like the Beatles had in Brian Epstein and George Martin. Many were immediately thrust into the deep waters of sudden fame, unfamiliar studios and producers, unchartered tour dates and unruly fan bases, internecine skirmishes among members, and the pressure to produce a follow-up single to the miracle first hit. All they knew about how to be a band was that the Beatles (to say nothing of the Monkees) made it look simple.

Even when a band's manager and producer turned out to be the father of the keyboard player who was the co-author of the band's first hit, it was no guarantee of longevity, or even another Top 10 hit. Such was the case with the Left Banke, whose ineffable "Walk Away Renee" was co-written by group member Michael Brown. Brown's manager/producer was his father Harry Lookofsky, a classical violinist whose influence gave rise to the song's sound and subsequent labeling as "baroque rock," noted for the inclusion of instruments such as flute and harpsichord. After writing their second single, the Top 20 hit, "Pretty Ballerina," Brown started exhibiting some profoundly anti-social behavior. Although both hits had been inspired by his unrequited love for his bass player's girlfriend, it was simply not acceptable for him to replace all the other members of the band with studio musicians for the next single, which was derailed by a lawsuit on behalf of the offended players.

After Brown quit the band, the Left Banke's career quickly dried up, leaving a lot of frustrated fans of baroque rock in their wake. But it was even more frustrating for fans of Michael Brown. His next move was as an unofficial part of the group Montage, producing and writing most of their self-titled 1969 album, which led off with "I Shall Call Her Mary," a track written about his new muse, Mary Weiss of the Shangri-Las. The album also included a cover

of the Left Banke's third single "Desiree." That year Brown reunited with the Left Banke's lead singer Steve Martin on a song called
"Myrah," which failed to chart. In 1971 Brown sang two songs in
the movie *Hot Parts* (backed by the Left Banke), "Love Songs in the
Night" and "Two by Two." With Ian Lloyd singing lead, Brown
was involved with the first *Stories* album, but left before their breakthrough hit of 1973, a Number One cover of Hot Chocolate's
"Brother Louie," which appeared on their second album *About Us*.
The mercurial Brown then moved on to the Beckies, whose only
album came out in 1976.

In 1966, folk rock was still the prevailing sound on the charts,
with groups shaped by the coffee house circuit making the transi-
tion to a new generation of rock theaters and clubs (Ciro's, the
Troubadour, and the Trip in L.A.; the Matrix and the Fillmore
in San Francisco; the Cafe Au Go Go, Electric Circus, and Fillmore East in New York City; and the Grande Ballroom in Detroit, among others). The movement was led by Dylan ("Rainy
Day Women #12 & 35," "I Want You"), along with groups such as
the Byrds ("Eight Miles High," "It Won't Be Wrong"), the Lovin'
Spoonful ("Daydream," "Summer in the City"), and Simon &
Garfunkel ("The Sounds of Silence," "I Am a Rock," "A Hazy
Shade of Winter"). Harmony-based vocal groups like the Mamas
and the Papas ("California Dreamin'," "Monday Monday") joined
the party, along with the Association ("Along Comes Mary"), the
Outsiders ("Time Won't Let Me"), the Grass Roots ("Where Were
You When I Needed You"), and the Cyrkle ("Red Rubber Ball").

Managed by Brian Epstein, the Cyrkle also toured with the Beatles in 1966, but, as with the Remains (and the Cryan' Shames, out
of Chicago) they didn't last for more than a year beyond their first
hit, with two founding members cutting out for the less competitive realms of jingle writing. The Mamas and the Papas received
a lot of ink as hippie scene makers; especially when John Phillips
helped put together the famed Monterey Pop Festival and Mama
Cass acted as Hollywood's ultimate hostess to the superstars. Still,
the jangly San Francisco band the Grass Roots actually had more
Top 40 hits.

Most of the other San Francisco bands drifted toward psychedelia, aided by the easy availability of LSD. By 1966, the Beau Brummels, one of the scene's pioneering British-sounding folk rock bands, was already on the commercial decline, having peaked in 1965 with "Laugh Laugh" and "Just a Little," both produced by Sylvester Stewart (aka Sly Stone) for the tiny Autumn label. Before going out on his own with Sly and the Family Stone, Stewart also produced "Dance with Me," the first single for the Mojo Men in 1965. Their next single, "Sit Down, I Think I Love You," written by Stephen Stills, made the Top 40 in 1967. The Beau Brummels dropped out of the singles market in 1966 after covering Bob Dylan's "One Too Many Mornings." The Sopwith Camel put out "Hello Hello" at the end of 1966, but were into an East Coast Lovin' Spoonful vibe, soon to be hopelessly out of fashion when the acid rock triumvirate of the Jefferson Airplane ("Somebody to Love," "White Rabbit"), Moby Grape ("Omaha"), and Country Joe and the Fish ("Not So Sweet Martha Lorraine") hit the charts in 1967, followed by Janis Joplin and Big Brother and the Holding Company ("Piece of My Heart") in 1968. The Grateful Dead, anchors of the scene, were too busy playing free concerts for Ken Kesey and the Merry Pranksters to worry about singles until "Uncle John's Band" de-virginized them in 1970. Singles were the province of garage rock bands like the Shadows of Knight, whose glorious "Gloria," written by Van Morrison, would be covered by the garage band universe. In 1965, the Leaves (featuring Dino Valenti) released "Hey Joe, Where You Gonna Go?" whose title was shortened to "Hey Joe" the following year, when it was recorded by Jimi Hendrix.

Acid rock, aka psychedelic rock or psychedelic pop, may have really started in 1966 in Austin, Texas, with Roky Erickson and his band, the Thirteenth Floor Elevators ("You're Gonna Miss Me"). This group toured with Grace Slick and the Great Society before Slick joined the Jefferson Airplane. (Janis Joplin considered joining the band before she left for San Francisco to sing with Big Brother and the Holding Company.) But sustained use of LSD and a marijuana possession charge got them into trouble. In 1969 Erickson chose to be committed to a mental hospital rather than face jail time. *Easter Everywhere* (1967) is generally considered their best album.

Also falling victim to drugs and musical indecision was Love, Arthur Lee's Byrds-influenced Beatlesque psychedelic rock band that lasted from 1966 to 1968. Their top single was "7 and 7 Is" (1966), but they were better known for two fine albums: *Da Capo* (1967) and *Forever Changes* (1968). Like the newly studio-bound Beatles, Love disdained touring, but the band quickly disintegrated after Bryan McLean, Lee's guitarist and collaborator, left due to a heroin addiction.

Other than Love, Los Angeles was sunshine city on the charts of 1967, with groups like Harpers Bizarre ("Come to the Sunshine"), the Turtles ("Happy Together"), the Yellow Balloon ("Yellow Balloon"), the Sunshine Company ("Happy"), the Peanut Butter Conspiracy ("It's a Happening Thing"), and the Merry-Go-Round ("Live"), mining the vibes put forth by the Beatles' 1967 singles output. Emitt Rhodes, founder of the Merry-Go-Round, would mine those vibes even further after he broke up the band to embark on a solo career, producing the very McCartneyesque album *Emitt Rhodes* in 1970.

Out of the dark side of the sunshine experience (sunshine was also the name of a type of acid) came the garage rock sound of the Seeds ("Pushin' Too Hard") and the psychedelic rock of the Strawberry Alarm Clock ("Incense and Peppermints") and Sagittarius ("My World Fell Down"), the latter group a studio creation of Gary Usher. The folk rock super group the Buffalo Springfield ("For What It's Worth") outgrew its humble Top 40 beginnings to produce future members of Poco and Crosby, Stills, Nash and Young. Harpers Bizarre, whose members included future Van Halen producer Ted Templeman, had one lone Top 20 hit: a cover of Paul Simon's "The 59th Street Bridge Song (Feelin' Groovy)." They were also fond of Van Dyke Parks' much-admired "High Coin." The Turtles had calmed down some since launching their career with a Dylan cover ("It Ain't Me Babe"), but they were still cool enough to release Harry Nilsson's "The Story of Rock and Roll" as a single.

By 1968, even the Beatles, safely ensconced at Abbey Road, were feeling those dark vibes, with the scary B side "I Am the Walrus" setting the tone at the end of 1967. The next year would find them unusually somber and philosophical, releasing "Lady Madonna" backed with "The Inner Light," followed by "Hey Jude" with the politically charged "Revolution" on the flip side. Their final three singles of the decade didn't get much brighter, all of them alluding to desperate times inside the castle walls, starting with Paul's plea to John to "Get Back," continuing with John's obstinate answer in "The Ballad of John and Yoko," and followed by the jarring use of the phrase "over me" by Lennon in "Come Together." Its B side, George Harrison's "Something," signaled George's imminent departure as well, like the once dependent spouse who suddenly starts to earn a living.

In 1970 the Beatles' two defining eulogies were released, "Let It Be" and "The Long and Winding Road," which were preceded by John's initial Plastic Ono Band efforts, the less-than- revolutionary political rallying cry "Give Peace a Chance," the harrowing "Cold Turkey," and the zeitgeist-defining "Instant Karma." By the end of the year, when George added "My Sweet Lord," the Beatles were over, Simon and Garfunkel were over, the Buffalo Springfield were over, the Monkees were long since over, the Lovin' Spoonful were over, the Mamas and the Papas were over, and the Byrds' career had ended with "Jesus Is Just Alright" (after being shot in the back in the somber "Ballad of Easy Rider," co-written by Bob Dylan). The Turtles' Top 40 career ended in 1970 with a re-release of "Eve of Destruction" (from their first album in 1965), which spent two weeks at number 100.

After abandoning the Beatlesque Nazz ("Hello It's Me") in 1969 and the Beatlesque Runt ("We Gotta Get You a Woman") in 1970, Todd Rundgren went solo with the Beatlesque LP *Something / Anything?* ("I Saw the Light") in 1972. After three Top 20 hits in two years ("Woodstock," "Teach Your Children," and "Ohio"), Crosby, Stills and Nash (and sometimes Young) broke apart into separate solo identities. The Spoonful's John Sebastian went solo. The Mothers of Invention's Frank Zappa went solo. Janis Joplin left Big Brother and the Holding Company to go solo. Alex Chilton left the Box Tops in search of the lost chord. Among the last of the American Beatles were Raspberries, arriving on the Cleveland scene in 1972 when the only Beatle clone around was the expatriate trio America ("A Horse with No Name," "I Need You," "Ventura Highway"). America was formed in London, and after self-producing their first three albums, handed the reins to George Martin for several more hits ("Tin Man," "Lonely People," "Sister Golden Hair," "Daisy Jane"). With no such connections and no such luck, Eric Carmen gave the world a thrilling blast of Beatlemania with "Go All the Way" in 1972 before lapsing into diminishing returns. Two years later, and still a year away from embarking on his own solo career, Carmen's parting shot with Raspberries was the prescient "Overnight Sensation (Hit Record)," which made the Top 20. But by then it was too late and Carmen went on to a Beatlesque solo career.

A much sadder case of wasted time and potential was that of Alex Chilton and Big Star. Emerging in Memphis with the Box Tops when he was a teenager in 1967, Chilton had already helped create iconic hits including "The Letter," "Cry Like a Baby," "I Met Her in Church," and "Soul Deep." Like the Beatles, Chilton was looking to expand beyond the teenybopper stage. After a meeting with the Byrds' Roger McGuinn in New York City, he returned to Memphis and formed Big Star with new songwriting partner Chris Bell. The result was *#1 Record*, released in the spring of 1972, and containing such perfect Beatlesque pop rock songs as "When My Baby's Beside Me," "Don't Lie to Me," "Thirteen" (based on seeing the Beatles), and "In the Street," which was later covered by Beatle fanatics Cheap Trick as the theme for the TV series *That 70s Show*. Due to label ineptitude and internal distribution problems, the album tanked. Incensed and depressed, Bell quit the band. *Radio City*, released early in 1974, had two of Chilton's finest songs, "Back of a Car" and "September Gurls," but it, too, was heard by almost no one except record critics, who got their records for free anyway. *Third / Sister Lovers*, completed at the end of 1974, consisted of moody epics like "Holocaust," but was considered too intricate and emotional for radio; the marketplace having by now gone way beyond anything even remotely resembling the American Beatles sound.

In its place were the original Beatles, now into their solo careers. McCartney issued eleven albums in the 1970s, including two solo efforts and nine with his group Wings. Lennon issued eight, four solo and four with the Plastic Ono Band. Harrison and Starr also issued eight albums apiece. This seemed sufficient enough to mollify the stranded, wounded hordes of Beatle fans, a small percentage of whom came out for Tom O'Horgan's off-Broadway show, *Sgt. Pepper's Lonely Hearts Club Band on the Road*, which played at the Beacon Theatre in New York City in 1974 and 1975. At this point, an obscure band called Klaatu attempted the previously unheard-of feat of becoming, for a brief, shimmering moment in 1976, the Canadian Beatles. But Klaatu's self-titled album (ironically recorded for Capitol) was revealed to be nothing but a slightly Beatlesque hype, although that notion alone propelled the Toronto group's two releases into the album Top 40, with the single "Sub Rosa Subway" making the Top 100 and "Calling Occupants of Interplanetary Craft" gaining a Top 40 cover by the Carpenters.

This distant whiff of Beatlemania was enough, however, to inspire Steve Leber and David Krebs, managers of Aerosmith, to fabricate an entire Broadway production called *Beatlemania* in 1977, a winningly clonelike spectacle that ran for over a thousand performances, surviving through 1979 before spawning several traveling companies, one of which even played London. The production eventually merged in the early eighties with a somewhat similar tribute concept called *Rain* that started in California and has continued to run ever since. Although *Beatlemania: The Album* was received as warmly by nostalgia buffs as the show, the original cast of Joe (Pecorino), Mitch (Weissman), Les (Fradkin), and Justin (McNeill) hardly had the same historical resonance as John, Paul, George, and Ringo. The 1981 film version, *Beatlemania: The Movie* proved to be a stiff.

But nowhere near as stiff as the film musical version of *Sgt. Pepper's Lonely Hearts Club Band* that appeared in 1978, for which George

Martin, as its musical director and producer of the soundtrack album, must be forever hanging his head in shame. Based on Tom O'Horgan's modest-by-comparison off-Broadway show, the film starred the Bee Gees: brothers Barry, Robin, and Maurice Gibb. Fresh from their disco reinvention in *Saturday Night Fever*, the brothers did a complete career 180 by regressing to their Beatle clone roots. The soundtrack featured twenty-one tracks from *Sgt Pepper* and *Abbey Road*, with the Bee Gees appearing on ten titles, including "Getting Better," "Good Morning, Good Morning," "She's Leaving Home," "Golden Slumbers / Carry That Weight" (with Peter Frampton), and "Because" (with Alice Cooper). Robin Gibb had a hit with "Oh! Darling," Earth, Wind and Fire scored with "Got to Get You into My Life," and Aerosmith did a credible job on "Come Together." In the spirit of re-creating the famous *Pepper* album cover, which had already been re-created to death (most notably by Frank Zappa), producer Robert Stigwood persuaded a huge number of otherwise unemployed C- and D-list celebrities to participate in the film. Among them, only Donovan, Peter Noone of Herman's Hermits, disgruntled Apple artist Jackie Lomax, and maybe Del Shannon ("From Me to You") had anything more than the most tenuous ties to the Beatles. Carole Channing? Chita Rivera? Connie Stevens? Gwen Verdon? Sha-Na-Na? Jim Dandy of Black Oak Arkansas? Leif Garrett? The saddest part of the whole fiasco was that it was supposed to be taken seriously.

Meanwhile, with the American psyche once again primed for Beatlemania, Rockford, Illinois' Cheap Trick was the first group to take advantage of it in 1977 with genuine hard rock fervor ("I Want You to Want Me," "Surrender") and Rick Nielsen's antic presence, contributing twisted lyrics and playing a series of wonderful guitars. Detroit-based the Romantics ("What I Like About You," "Talking in Your Sleep"), and Northern California's Tommy Tutone ("867-5309 / Jenny") mined the skinny tie look and perfect pop predilections. Todd Rundgren was even more overt with his new outfit Utopia, producing 1979's homage to the Fab Four *Deface the Music*, a masterful tribute to all the myriad facets of the Beatles' musical development. Coming a little late to the party was Dick

Clark, who helmed the fictional documentary *The Birth of the Beatles* (1979), which contained upwards of twenty early tracks, including two versions of "I Saw Her Standing There" (one with Ringo on drums and one with Pete Best), "Blue Suede Shoes," "Lawdy Miss Clawdy" (performed by Rory Storm), and a lot of Little Richard and Chuck Berry covers, culminating with "P.S. I Love You" and "Love Me Do."

With all this cool, crass, overt, and latent Beatlemania in the air, it would seem the 1980s would be ripe for a full-scale return to the kind of jangly, melodic songs pioneered and inspired by the Beatles. To some degree this happened. But not for reasons anyone anticipated.

James Taylor, circa 1970s.

10

APPLE RECORDS

Perhaps the most obvious initial showcase for both the music that influenced the Beatles and the music they influenced (apart from their individual and group efforts) is the output from Apple Records (1968 to 1973) and its even shorter-lived Zapple subsidiary (a cheeky nod to Frank Zappa's Bizarre Label), which only released two records, John and Yoko's *Unfinished Music No. 2: Life with the Lions* and George's *Electronic Music*. But bizarre is the only word to describe the random assortment of signings that took place at the wildly mismanaged label in the waning years of the 1960s. The only element more bizarre was the daily workings of the label itself, a perfect expression of the generally demented atmosphere of unlimited money, drugs, naïveté, and entitlement that permeated the Beatles' camp.

Apple served partly as a vanity press for all the Beatles' personal indulgences, including John's tape recorded indiscretions with Yoko, George's early efforts on the Moog, and Ringo's nostalgic fling with pop standards. In view of this, it was surprising that Apple had as much success as it did. Keeping things in the family, the Beatles named Peter Asher (Jane's brother, of Peter and Gordon fame), as head of A&R, a position he would keep even after Paul and Jane broke up. One of his first signings was an unknown folk rocker from Boston named James Taylor, who was then living in England. Taylor's self-titled album, released in December 1968, contained several memorable tunes, including "Sunshine Sunshine," "Rainy Day Man," and "Carolina in My Mind," the latter featuring McCartney on bass and an uncredited George Harrison singing backup. George got an extra special boost from the album, using Taylor's "Something in the Way She Moves" as the first line of his breakout song "Something." Fitting in perfectly with the prevailing zeitgeist, Taylor was hospitalized for drug treatments and sent back to America at the time of his sole Apple release, and was thus unable to promote it. That his career at Apple lasted for only the one album was a costly music industry anomaly; an example of either Apple's complete lack of business smarts or their advanced sense of themselves as a loose, artist-friendly collective, with contracts being a part of the older order (i.e., passé). In either case, once on Warner Bros., Taylor immediately zoomed to stardom as a prime mover in the new, mellow singer-songwriter era along with Brill Building graduate Carole King.

Inundated by tapes from every hopeful on the continent, Apple signed artists chiefly based on the suggestions of friends. The first and only Number One single that didn't have a Beatle attached to it was by Welsh folk singer Mary Hopkin, who was recommended to Paul McCartney by svelte supermodel Twiggy, who happened to catch her on the TV talent competition *Opportunity Knocks*. Produced by Paul, the song that was selected might have come straight from the ancient songbag of the Quarrymen. "Those Were the Days" was based on old Russian folk tune that had been translated and updated by Gene Raskin. Although it had been a staple in the repertoire of the folk group the Limeliters since 1962, it's possible that McCartney heard the song after reverting to his old Beatles habit of flipping through singles, finding it on the B side of an Engelbert Humperdinck hit, "The Last Waltz," which had held the top spot in the UK for five weeks in 1967. The Beatles' pedigree at the time was so strong that Hopkin's version easily withstood a cover by Sandie Shaw that came out a month or so later, which failed to chart in either the UK or the U.S. (It did, however, make the Top 40 in Australia.) Hopkins' version hit Number One in the UK and Number 2 in the U.S. Her follow-up was a Lennon and McCartney tune that the Beatles never recorded called "Goodbye," which peaked at Number 2.

Her last hit, "Knock Knock Who's There," came in second in the Eurovision Song Contest in 1970.

The Apple signings were basically the province and playground of the mercurial tastes of Paul and George, with John and Ringo represented to a lesser extent. The first four Apple singles were released simultaneously. Two were hits: the Beatles' "Hey Jude" and Hopkin's "Those Were the Days." The other two were unmitigated flops: "Sour Milk Sea" by Jackie Lomax (a tune George Harrison abandoned at "The White Album" sessions) and "Thingumybob," a brass band version of Paul McCartney's theme for the TV show of the same name, played by the well-known Black Dyke Mills Band, with "Yellow Submarine" on the B side.

"Sour Milk Sea," which George wrote in Rishikesh, reflected George's familiar Indian philosophy but the title might have been one of the most unappealing ever given a single. The record didn't exactly jump-start the already stalled career of Lomax, a transplanted British soul singer who had been a friend of the extended Beatle family since Brian Epstein brought him back from America in 1967. After Epstein died, Harrison stepped in as his surrogate musical guru. One would think that with George producing and a band consisting of Eric Clapton on guitar, McCartney on drums, Ringo on bass, and Nicky Hopkins on keyboards, the record could have transcended its title on credibility alone. But it failed to chart, and neither did the revealingly titled album *Is This What You Want?*, released in the spring of 1969. Lomax was soon back in America, picking up the pieces of what remained of his career.

The label's next discovery, the Iveys, fared a good deal better, although not at first. The band, which featured songwriters Tom Evans and Pete Ham, was brought to Apple by the Beatles' loyal but underpaid road manager and go-fer Mal Evans (no relation to Tom). The Beatlesque "Maybe Tomorrow" was the Iveys' first release, but since it only charted well in three countries, Allen Klein, who had just been brought in to unravel the mess at Apple, decided to release their album *Maybe Tomorrow*, only in West Germany, Japan, and Italy (although it had gone to Number One in Holland). A year later, the band, renamed Badfinger, recorded McCartney's

"Come and Get It," which became a huge transatlantic hit, spurred by its appearance in the Peter Sellers/Ringo Starr movie *The Magic Christian* along with two other Iveys songs, "Rock of Ages" and "Carry on Till Tomorrow." Badfinger's first album capitalized on the success of "Come and Get It" without it being the actual soundtrack. Essentially, *Magic Christian Music* was a re-release of the quickly deleted Iveys album that included "Maybe Tomorrow." Their second album, *No Dice*, contained another worldwide hit, "No Matter What" and a future pop standard "Without You," which quirky singer/songwriter and future Lennon drinking buddy Harry Nilsson brought to the top of the charts in 1972, the same year Badfinger's hit "Day After Day" peaked at number four, "Without You" was also covered by Mariah Carey in 1994. Presaging the fate of nearly every other Apple artist (aside from the four ex-Beatles), Badfinger ended badly, with both Pete Ham and Tom Evans committing suicide (Ham in 1975 and Evans in 1983). In 1976, original mentor Mal Evans was shot to death by police, who thought he was brandishing a loaded rifle during a domestic dispute.

In general, 1969 was as bad a year at Apple as it was for the imploding Beatles. Singles by non-entities called Trash ("Road to Nowhere," followed up by a cover of "Golden Slumbers / Carry That Weight") and Brute Force ("King of Fuh") competed with an obvious Harrison signing, the Radha Krishna Temple ("Hare Krishna Mantra"), and future UK superstars Hot Chocolate ("Give Peace a Chance") for the dubious honor of most disappointing record. The woefully out-of-place Modern Jazz Quartet released their second of two mediocre albums, *Space*, which followed *Under the Jasmine Tree* to the cut-out bins. Little Richard and Ray Charles keyboard player Billy Preston broke the trend with "That's the Way God Planned It," which fell short of making the UK Top 10. Aside from *Abbey Road*, the rest of Apple's time was taken up with assorted Beatle solo projects, including John and Yoko's *Wedding Album*, the Plastic Ono Band's *Live Peace in Toronto 1969*, Ringo's *Sentimental Journey*, and in April 1970, Paul McCartney's debut solo album *McCartney*, delivered just prior to the release of the Beatles' last album, *Let It Be*.

Produced by George Harrison, "That's the Way God Planned

It" could have been a knockout, considering the superstar backup band Harrison assembled behind the always stellar Preston, which included Eric Clapton on guitar, Keith Richards on bass, Ginger Baker on drums, and Doris Troy singing backup. But neither the title tune nor its follow up, "Everything's Alright," gave it any momentum. Preston stuck around, however, for a second album, *Encouraging Words*, which may have been one of his best. On this record, George gave Preston the honor of recording two songs he was planning to use on his first solo album, "All Things Must Pass" and a song Harrison would take to the top by the end of the year, "My Sweet Lord." Preston also collaborated with Harrison on "Sing One for the Lord," and just to be on the politically safe side, he covered Lennon and McCartney's "I've Got a Feeling" in amazing fashion. When this also flopped, Preston escaped to A&M, where his career would soar.

Thanks to the Preston connection and a burgeoning career in England as a backup singer, Doris Troy landed the mixed blessing of having an Apple release as well. Known for co-writing and singing "Just One Look" in 1963 (covered by Linda Ronstadt, the Hollies, Anne Murray, Lulu, and Harry Nilsson, among others), Troy and her eponymous Apple album also benefitted from the Beatles' good name by being able to assemble stellar sidemen, among them Peter Frampton, Stephen Stills, Eric Clapton, Leon Russell, and Delaney and Bonnie. (The latter's 1969 Apple album, *Accept No Substitute*, was cancelled, to their subsequent delight, and released on Elektra, where it made the U.S. album charts.) On her self-titled album, Doris Troy showed exemplary taste in covers (Stephen Stills' "Special Care" and Joe South's "Games People Play"), but the single releases of "Ain't That Cute" and "Jacob's Ladder" (the latter with "Get Back" as its B side) went nowhere.

In 1971, Apple moved full scale into the movie soundtrack business with three initial releases. *Raga* was a straight documentary based on the life of sitar master Ravi Shankar. Produced by Ringo, *Cometogether* was a vanity project for director Saul Swimmer, who had previously lensed the Beatle documentary *Let It Be* and would go on to greater glory with his filming of George's *The Concert for*

Bangladesh. The soundtrack album for *Cometogether* included the hit single "I Can Sing a Rainbow / Love Is Blue" by the Dells, but nothing by the Youngbloods, whose music was in the movie. The blockbuster of the three was the cult classic *El Topo (the Mole).* One of the original "midnight movies," predating *The Rocky Horror Picture Show* by four years, this surreal film influenced a number of important tastemakers of the era, including David Lynch, John Lennon, and Bob Dylan. Lynch would later apply his twisted cinematic sense to television's *Twin Peaks.* Dylan would go on to star in the similar *Pat Garrett and Billy the Kid* (from whence came the brilliant "Knockin' on Heaven's Door"). John Lennon would commission British classical pianist and arranger John Barham, who worked with George on *Wonderwall Music* and *All Things Must Pass,* to re-record *El Topo*'s score as written by the film's director and star, Alejandro Jodorowsky. The film played in art houses for years, principally for fans of the acid western genre, which included (in addition to *Pat Garrett and Billy the Kid) The Shooting* (1966), *Easy Rider* (1969), *Two Lane Blacktop* with James Taylor (1971), and *Greaser's Palace* (1972).

Apple's other foray into the classical realm resulted in two albums by British composer John Tavener, including his first important piece, *The Whale,* based on the biblical story of Jonah, which was premiered at the London Sinfonietta in 1968 and released on Apple in 1970. *Celtic Requiem,* featuring soprano June Barton, followed the next year.

One of the highlights of 1971, in a strictly countercultural sense, was "God Save Us" (originally "God Save Oz"), written and demoed by John Lennon (co-authored by Yoko) with the single release performed by Bill Elliott and the Elastic Oz Band. The song was written to protest the obscenity trial of the editors of the British underground magazine *Oz* for their May 1970 *Schoolkidz Oz* issue. In an example of the repressive times following the fall of Aquarius, the editors were found guilty (much like the Chicago Seven), but were acquitted on appeal. Yoko issued the original demo in *The John Lennon Anthology,* released in 1998.

On a musical basis, the year belonged to two female singers of totally opposite styles and sensibilities, who endured a totally different experience at Apple. Ronnie Spector was a longtime Beatle favorite and one of the greatest voices in rock 'n' roll history. The imprisoned wife of eccentric producer Phil Spector, the former Ronette recorded one single for the label, George's "Try Some, Buy Some," which was co-produced by Harrison and Phil, who was now the new head of A&R at Apple after completing the infamous *Let It Be* remix. The record, however, found Ronnie Spector tragically miscast in mood and message. George later put the song on his album *Living Spirits in the Material World*, using the same arrangement. David Bowie covered it on 2003's *Reality*. (John Lennon was especially partial to the song's B side, "Tandoori Chicken.")

After failing at Apple, Ronnie met a similar fate in the years after her divorce from Phil, as she attempted to make a comeback. Her magnificent take on Billy Joel's "Say Goodbye to Hollywood," with Bruce Springsteen and the E Street Band, backed with Miami Steve Van Zandt's "Baby Please Don't Go," failed to chart in 1977. In 1980 *Siren* was produced by girl group sound aficionado Genya Ravan (Goldie and the Gingerbreads and Ten Wheel Drive), which featured the Ramones' "Here Today, Gone Tomorrow." Ronnie's 1986 cameo with Eddie Money on "Take Me Home Tonight" led to 1987's *Unfinished Business* (living up to its title); the Desmond Child track "Love on a Rooftop" became famous primarily for inspiring Child to write similar future hits for Bon Jovi. Joey Ramone would be back in 1999 to produce *She Talks to Rainbows*, an album (released in Australia only) famous for Ronnie's legendary version of "Don't Worry Baby," a song originally written for her by Brian Wilson.

The other female voice belonged, of course, to Yoko Ono, although here the word "voice" fails to do justice to the range of sounds and feelings conveyed by the singer, in turn ethereal and hellish, impossible to listen to, and impossible to resist. Her first album, the experimental, atmospheric, and just plain weird *Yoko Ono / Plastic Ono Band*, is the soundtrack to a ritual sacrifice. Released at the end of 1970, it featured Ornette Coleman on the second side's opening track, "AOS." Two other tracks became Lennon B sides, the scathing "Why" (which backed "Mother") and "Touch Me" (which backed "Power to the People"). "Greenfield Morning (I Pushed an Empty Baby Carriage All Over the City)" was an early leap into noise rock.

On her 1971 double album *Fly*, Yoko's focus exploded with the sixteen-minute "Mind Train," which dominated the first side, and the twenty-three-minute "Fly" dominating the second. "Don't Worry Kyoko (Mummy's Only Looking for Her Hand in the Snow")," the B side of "Cold Turkey," is here in all its frenzied glory. The keen-like "Mind Holes" is the soundtrack to a Japanese acid western, but "Midsummer New York" is a relatively straight-ahead rocker. The standout track is the grim and haunting "Mrs. Lennon," which would lend its aura to Alex Chilton's "Holocaust," as performed by Big Star on *Sister Lovers* from 1974.

The third album, *Approximately Infinite Universe*, backed by the New York City rock band Elephant's Memory, came out early in 1973, with twenty-four discrete tracks, including the poignant "Song for John" (the feminist's answer to Helen Reddy), "What a Mess" (which equates abortion to masturbation), "Death of Samantha" (in which Yoko sounds eerily like Kate Bush), and the R&B-flavored "I Felt Like Smashing My Face in a Clear Glass Window" (in which Yoko confronts her split with John, which would last until 1975). The subject dominates her final Apple album *Feeling the Space*, in which she vents with spleen and gusto on such tracks as "Run, Run, Run," "Angry Young Woman," and "Woman Power." Combined, her four albums spent a total of nine weeks on the *Billboard* chart, but during those weeks, women with exotic sensibilities as varied as Lene Lovich, Sinead O'Connor, and Bjork were obviously listening.

Elephant's Memory got to make their own album for Apple in 1972, while Ringo's favorite, Chris Hodge, only released a couple of singles: "We're on Our Way" and "Goodbye Sweet Lorraine." The Sundown Playboys, a Cajun band from Louisiana, had one single, "Saturday Night Special," which came in through the slush pile. Although Elephant's Memory had achieved a bit of prior fame for placing two songs in the film *Midnight Cowboy* ("Jungle Gym at the Zoo" and "Old Man Willow"), their self-titled Apple album did little to sustain their momentum. They can also be heard backing John Lennon on half of *Some Time in New York City*. On the other half, John jams with his favorite Beatles antagonists, Frank Zappa's Mothers of Invention.

One of the last Apple signings was that of two brothers from New Jersey, Lon and Derrek van Eaton. Their album *Brothers*, released in September 1972, got lost in the shuffle of the breakups and lawsuits that split the band and the label apart. Unfortunately, *The Pope Smokes Dope*, released in April 1972 by David Peel and the Lower East Side, did see the light of day. Reflecting John Lennon's belated attempt to join the radical element at the butt end of the Revolution, Peel's singsong street polemics (already well established in *Have a Marijuana* and *The American Revolution*) fit all too well into Lennon's limited but still antic sense of political theater. With an offensively simplistic presentation, the always exhibitionistic Peel's songs rarely went beyond their obvious titles. Thus, potentially revealing subjects like "I'm a Runaway," "Chicago Conspiracy," "Ballad of New York City / John Lennon and Yoko Ono," "Bob Dylan," and the "Okie from Muskogee" parody "Hippie from New York City" merely revel in their idiocy, and in so doing, ironically paint a portrait of an era and a revolution headed for a crack-up.

As with the Beatles, it was a crack-up John Lennon seemed to be perversely looking forward to.

The Sex Pistols.

11

THE ANTI-BEATLES

In his induction speech for Jimmy Page at the Rock and Roll Hall of Fame ceremonies in New York City in 1994, U2 guitarist Dave Evans, otherwise known as the Edge, admitted, "We spent a lot of years in the garage trying to sound like anyone other than Jimmy Page."

By the 1980s, young musicians in fledgling rock bands had already had more than enough of Page's signature riffs in Led Zeppelin. Although they never released a single in the UK and had only one Top 10 hit in the U.S. ("Whole Lotta Love"), they'd been the preeminent rock band since their arrival in 1969. Their arena-sized sound and badass image had been imprinted upon a generation of headbanging, hotel room trashing, heavy metal bands throughout the world, even without the help of MTV. Over the course of ten years, while their 1972 epic "Stairway to Heaven" had long since replaced "Louie Louie" and "Johnny B. Goode" as the essential rite of lead guitar passage, other extravaganzas like "Dazed and Confused," "All My Love," "Good Times, Bad Times," "Heartbreaker," "The Lemon Song," "Going to California," "Ramble On," and "Kashmir" from their nine regular albums made them impossible to avoid, if not abjectly imitate. (The combined sales of these albums were over eighty-nine times platinum.) Thus, to make any sort of mark as an original band with a guitar player in it required a total deconstruction if not demolition of Page: the man, the player, and the myth.

But this is how eras change in rock music, when the young finally declare their independence from their older brother's rock 'n' roll by setting fire to the legends and dancing amid the cinders.

Which is not to say Jimmy Page had this in mind in 1969 when he gladly did the two-step on the Beatles' grave, supplanting them in the U.S. and England as the top band in the land. The emergence of Led Zeppelin from the ruins of the always underappreciated Yardbirds must have delighted not just Page, but his compatriots on the British blues scene, who were rendered obsolete the minute the Beatles internationalized the Merseybeat craze. More likely, he was just taking the next evolutionary step following Clapton's Cream and Townshend's Who, mixing the power of the blues with the super power of the Marshall stack to impress the boys, and with Robert Plant as lead singer throwing in some crotch-grabbing teenybop moves, impressing the young girls as well. The fact they ratcheted up the Beatles' Middle Eastern Maharishi yearnings with references to demented mystic Alistair Crowley was only icing on the cake. The fact that Ozzy Osbourne emerged like a behemoth from the moors of Birmingham a year later in Black Sabbath, upping the heavy metal ante in *Black Sabbath* ("N.I.B.," "The Wizard," "Black Sabbath"), *Paranoid* ("Paranoid," "Iron Man," "War Pigs") and *Master of Reality* ("Children of the Grave") past antisocial and into the realms of the psychotic was just the cherry on top.

But the anti-Beatles reaction had been planted in the populace way before that. At first, all Bob Dylan fans were de facto anti-Beatles, although Dylan himself claimed to be an early convert to their thrilling innocence. But the more rabid folkies who eventually disowned Dylan for his move to electricity only saw the Beatles as plastic pop. Frank Zappa lampooned them in *We're Only in It for the Money*, soon after *Sgt. Pepper*, but Zappa lampooned everything, and the album was more a commentary on flower power than the Beatles. But the fact that the Beatles aligned themselves so closely with the prevailing hippie culture of acid, love beads, and meditation made them ripe to take the hit for all the excesses of their era and to effectively take the era down with them when they disintegrated.

If Led Zeppelin was noisier than the Beatles ever hoped to be, it was the Velvet Underground that really stood in opposition to everything the Beatles represented. "Let's say we were a little bit sarcastic about the love thing," said founding member Lou Reed. "They thought acid was going to solve everything. You take acid and you solve the problems of the universe. And we just said, 'Bullshit. You people are fucked. That's not the way it is and you're kidding yourself.'"

Far from thinking heroin was the answer, Lou Reed nonetheless wrote anthems for a drug subculture that was anything but loving and peaceful on their first album *The Velvet Underground and Nico*, released in 1967, which included early nods to the decadent decade that was to follow. "Heroin," "I'm Waiting for the Man," and "Black Angel's Death Song" were leavened only by bittersweet morning-after hangover laments like "Femme Fatale," "Sunday Morning," and "I'll Be Your Mirror." In Nico they found a voice as ghostly and forbidding as Janis was earthy and Grace was cool. That same year, Nico put out *Chelsea Girls*, the desultory title track coming from an experimental film by Andy Warhol about the legendary bohemian enclave, the Chelsea Hotel. The album also contained probably the first version of Jackson Browne's classic lament "These Days," the rare Dylan treasure "I'll Keep It with Mine," and Tim Hardin's searching "Eulogy to Lenny Bruce," a kind of bookend to "European Son: To Delmore Schwartz" from the Velvets' first album. References to black comedy and dead poets (Schwartz died in 1966) aligned the band much closer to the Beats than the Beatles (or the hippies). Like Reed, Jack Kerouac came to despise the love generation (for co-opting his sacred message in his ultimate manifesto, *On the Road*, for their own heedless purposes).

As much as the Rolling Stones had been historically seen as the only true anti-Beatles group since their inception, this was really more of a ploy to keep their separate publicists busy. Maybe they didn't vacation together on the same yachts, but theirs was basically a healthy competition, highlighted by the Stones' 1969 album *Let It Bleed*, an accidentally witty takeoff on the Beatles' *Let It Be*, which it beat to the marketplace by six months. While *Let It Be* and *Abbey Road* were remote affairs, connected less to the end of an era than to the end of the Beatles, *Let It Bleed*, released a day before the tragic death at the Altamont concert, consciously or not document-ed the violence of a bloody year on the streets and campuses and even at the outdoor rock festivals of the world. "You Can't Always Get What You Want," the B side of the non-album "Honky Tonk Women," stands in stark contrast to the Beatles' much more naïve "All You Need Is Love."

The Stones' emergence, marked by 1968's *Beggar's Banquet* ("Stray Cat Blues," "Salt of the Earth," "Sympathy for the Devil") as men of, by, and for the people also contrasts with the Beatles of this era, who were far from the people, either convening with their guru in India or arguing with each other in the recording studio. When both bands finally decided to confront the bloody politics of that defining year, it was the Stones who beat the Beatles to the American singles charts by a week with "Street Fighting Man," put-ting it on the A side, while the Beatles relegated the tamer sounding "Revolution" to the B side. And even without the Beatles to kick around, the Stones found plenty of motivation in their newly found songwriting chops, with "Brown Sugar," "Wild Horses," "Bitch," "Sister Morphine," and "Dead Flowers" (from 1971's *Sticky Fingers*) moving them squarely into Velvet Underground musical and lyri-cal territory.

By the end of 1970, the Velvet Underground was seriously imploding, Beatles style, with co-founder John Cale leaving after 1968's *White Light / White Heat* ("Sister Ray," "I Heard Her Call My Name") and Lou Reed leaving in 1970 after writing two of the band's most enduring tracks, "Sweet Jane" and "Rock and Roll," for the ironically titled *Loaded* (as in "loaded" with hits). Like many in the ranks of the deposed folk rock era he ridiculed, Reed started his solo career in 1972 with *Lou Reed*, produced by Richard Robin-son, who'd previously worked with Flamin' Groovies on *Flamingo*. Later that year, *Transformer* came out, produced by David Bowie and Mick Ronson, with the fluke hit single "Walk on the Wild Side," a veritable 1968 flashback.

Any certified 1968 flashback would also have to include two anti-Beatle bands from Detroit, both signed by Elektra Records on the same day. The MC5, managed by John Sinclair, radical leader of the White Panthers, went in for blatant political diatribes on *Kick out the Jams* like "Motor City Is Burning" and the hit single "Kick out the Jams," which they performed, expletives included, on the lawn of the International Amphitheatre in Chicago, where the 1968 Democratic National Convention was being staged. Thus, they were too topical to last and too political to appeal to anyone but Weathermen sympathizers. The Psychedelic Stooges, fronted by James Osterberg (aka Iggy Pop) were a different case. Sensing the shift in public temperament away from blissful optimism, they dropped Psychedelic from their name, leaving a timeless mix of rock 'n' roll dupes of the counterculture and the Three Stooges. Blasting into 1969 with anthems to cosmic ennui like "1969," "No Fun," and "I Wanna Be Your Dog" (from *The Stooges*), they completely undid the Beatle ethos of harmony (both inner and outer, to say nothing of musical). Disdaining the intellectual pretensions of a Lou Reed and thumbing their noses at the virtuosic aura of a Jimmy Page, the ragged, hungry, shameless Stooges established for the ages the nihilistic anything-goes punk ethos that would dominate the hearts of many rock 'n' roll musicians and fans from then on. The Sex Pistols, avatars of England's punk renaissance of 1976-77, covered "No Fun" on their first album. In 1970 *Fun House* followed ("Loose," "TV Eye," "L.A. Blues," "Dirt"). Plagued by low sales, their classic *Raw Power* ("Search and Destroy") from 1973 was their final effort before Iggy Pop went solo in 1977 with *The Idiot*; a prodigal son returning in the midst of the punk renaissance.

While the Stooges were too short-lived and commercially limited to do any immediate damage, by far the most visible and virulent anti-Beatle musician on the planet in 1969 was someone with a unique insider's knowledge of the whole schtick from the very beginning: John Lennon.

If it wasn't the worldly if not otherworldly Japanese artist Yoko Ono who turned John against his childhood pals (as many women in a romantic relationship will do), it was inevitable that either John or Paul would outgrow the claustrophobic hell on Earth they'd created with the Beatles. As competitive as they always were, especially with each other, it was only a question of who would quit first. Unlike the TV show *Bewitched*, where you could simply cast another Darren in the place of the departed Darren, it would have been impossible for the Beatles to exist without either of their two creative driving forces.

And so, while John was doing everything he could to antagonize his former blood brothers by instituting Yoko as a virtual member of group, by introducing the fellows to the crass accountant Allen Klein, by inviting the mercurial Phil Spector into the mix, and by constantly threatening to make the Plastic Ono Band his full-time gig, it was actually Paul, pushed to the brink once too often, who made his exit public first, infuriating John.

While still with the Beatles, John used the Plastic Ono Band as a vehicle for his ragged performance of mainly rock 'n' roll oldies at the Toronto Peace Festival. *Live Peace in Toronto 1969* did feature Yoko's vocal pyrotechnics on "Don't Worry Kyoko" and John's admission of heroin use in "Cold Turkey." But by the time of his next album, *John Lennon/Plastic Ono Band*, the Beatles had broken up, and John found it more of a receptacle for his myriad confessions ("Mother," "My Mummy's Dead," "God," "Love," Working Class Hero"). Sufficiently cleansed, he then directed his anger toward his former partner in *Imagine*, released in 1971. Hidden behind the utopian sentiments of the title song were the lethal mortar blasts of "How Do You Sleep," featuring George Harrison on slide guitar. This song was apparently written in answer to Paul's own Lennon-bashing "Too Many People," the B side of the 1971 hit "Uncle Albert / Admiral Halsey," also found on *Ram*. True to form, Ringo's take on the breakup was a bit more accommodating in "Early 1970," the B side of the 1971 hit "It Don't Come Easy." Reserving all his B sides for Yoko, Lennon added scathing attacks to his album *Imagine*; "Crippled Inside," "Gimme Some Truth," and "Jealous Guy" further decimated the Beatle myth of godlike perfection. *Some Time in New York City*, released in 1972, smashed in the headstone, with MC5-like political rants about John Sinclair, Angela Davis, Attica, the troubles in Northern Ireland, and the plight of women, dark but relevant stuff the Beatles never would have touched. A few years later, British bands like the Sex Pistols

("God Save the Queen") and the Clash ("London Calling") would make provocative political statements *de rigueur* in the nascent punk scene of 1976.

Before he stepped aside in 1974 to allow the punks space to further mock the Beatles, John Lennon would first have to leave Yoko to get some space of his own. Mitigated a bit by Yoko's stage-managing of the affair from New York City, Lennon's year-and-a-half drunken sojourn to L.A. at least attracted some interesting musical bedfellows, among them Harry Nilsson, who'd been befriended by the Beatles as far back in 1967 when they declared the Pepperesque *Pandemonium Shadow Show* their favorite album of the year. The album featured "Cuddly Toy" (recorded by the Monkees), "Ten Little Indians" (a single by the Yardbirds), and a cogent rendition of "She's Leaving Home," the *Pepper* track that caused Brian Wilson such heartache. Naturally enough, in between trashing hotels and getting thrown out of nightclubs, Lennon produced Nilsson's 1974 mishmash of an album *Pussy Cats*, which included covers of songs by Dylan, Jimmy Cliff, the Drifters, and Bill Haley and His Comets.

Sufficiently chastened, Lennon was summoned home by Yoko in 1975 to father a child and get himself back together. But before he semi-retired from the scene, he tacitly endorsed the theatrics of former folkie David Bowie, now the crown prince of a prominent anti-Beatles movement called glam, by collaborating with him on the 1975 single "Fame," which became Bowie's first U.S. Number One hit.

With a dash of makeup, a touch of glitter, a bit of lipstick, and teased hair to match the Shangri-Las in their prime, a number of early 1970s bands took the "are you a boy or are you a girl?" accusations of the mid-sixties to flamboyant lengths in order to satirize them. Even Mick Jagger adopted this look for a while. The New York Dolls tried to get away with this on the streets of New York in 1973, but luckily they were based in Greenwich Village and had the streetwise chops to back up their outrageous performances. Songs like "Trash," "Personality Crisis," and "Looking for a Kiss" (from their first album *New York Dolls*, produced by Todd Rundgren) confirmed this. When they got Shadow Morton to produce their second album, those who knew his prior relationship to the sacred Shangri-Las were moved to the point of grateful tears. To them, *Too Much Too Soon* didn't disappoint ("Human Being," "Stranded in the Jungle," "There's Gonna Be a Showdown"). The trouble was, nobody else bought it. Soon, guitarist Johnny Thunders left the band and formed the Heartbreakers with punk scene pioneer Richard Hell (who had departed from Television) and former Dolls drummer Jerry Nolan. Formed in 1975, the band took two years to land a record deal, which happened only after Malcolm McLaren, the mad mastermind behind the Sex Pistols and a big Dolls fan, got them a gig touring with England's reigning punk royals: the Sex Pistols, the Clash, and the Damned. Unfortunately, the tour ended before it could even start, but the Heartbreakers' record *L.A.M.F.* came out on the Track label, featuring "Chinese Rocks" (written by Dee Dee Ramone and Richard Hell) and "Born Too Loose." From the Dolls, lead singer David Johansen went on to a career as a popular entertainer (usually dressed in men's clothes). In 1991, Johnny Thunders, a long-time heroin addict, died under mysterious circumstances.

By the time the Heartbreakers made their album, glam had already given way to punk as the best anti-Beatles response going. American bands like Alice Cooper and Kiss distilled the camp satire for mass consumption as if it were a rock 'n' roll musical (e.g., the tribal travesty *Hair*). Former Zappa signee Cooper went heavy on the ghoulish eye shadow and featured ritual beheadings as part of his act. Kiss dressed up as fully realized comic book characters, breathing fire and spitting blood. But only David Bowie went so far as to become his own alter ego in his personal rock opera, in the role of a lifetime as Ziggy Stardust (modeled on Iggy Pop and Lou Reed), who first appeared in 1972's *The Rise and Fall of Ziggy Stardust and the Spiders from Mars* ("Starman," "Suffragette City"). In 1972, Bowie provided glam with its defining anthem, "All the Young Dudes," a Top 10 hit in England that he wrote for Mick Ronson's band Mott the Hoople. It appeared on their fifth album *All the Young Dudes*. Ronson and Bowie produced Lou Reed's 1972 album *Transformer* ("Walk on the Wild Side," "Vicious") on which Lou appears to be wearing eyeliner on the cover.

In America, glam turned into arena rock relatively quickly, as working class heterosexuality reclaimed the music. But in effete Merry Olde England the genre reigned until punk obliterated it in the hearts of the musically obsessed; for everyone else, it remained extremely popular. In fact, some of the original glam acts went on to become the biggest hit makers of the decade. Gary Glitter, for instance had twelve Top 10 hits in the 1970s. Marc Bolan's T-Rex had eleven. The Sweet had ten. Bigger than all of them, Slade had thirteen, but they were really closer to the heavy metal offshoot known as sludge than glam. Not to be outdone, David Bowie had twelve hits (adding eleven more in the 1980s, including "Under Pressure," a duet with Queen). Queen wound up with eighteen Top 10 hits, but only eight of them came in the 1970s. The quint-essentially well-groomed Roxy Music (featuring Bryan Ferry) had ten Top 10 hits, but four of them came in the 1980s (Ferry had four Top 10 solo hits and one more in the eighties), by which time glam had morphed into early dance music and electronica.

Dance music and electronica were the last things on the mind of the four non-brothers who formed Ramones in 1974, their name itself tweaking Paul McCartney's stage name in the Silver Beatles ("Paul Ramon," a name he also used as a sideman on two 1969 Steve Miller tracks, "My Dark Hour" and "Celebration Song"). If their look was mock-Beatles, their songs and their whole attitude was a mockery of the fat cat FM radio / arena sound of long guitar and drum solos and introspective lyrics brought on by too much money and too much LSD. It was more like a leap backward to the rockabilly rage of Gene Vincent. If Ramones were the anti-Beatles, by their time of their first album in 1976, they were the anti-Led Zeppelin as well. As a concept it was a home run, even if *Ramones*, featuring "Blitzkrieg Bop," "Beat on the Brat," "Judy Is a Punk," and "Now I Wanna Sniff Some Glue," was more like the commercial equivalent of a bloop single.

Not surprisingly, Ramones were welcomed by the rising, raging punk movement in England, where they opened for Flamin'

Groovies and were befriended by the Clash and the Sex Pistols. Subsequent seventies albums: *Leave Home* ("Gimme Gimme Shock Treatment," "Sheena Is a Punk Rocker," "Pinhead"), *Rocket to Russia* ("Rockaway Beach," "Teenage Lobotomy"), *Road to Ruin* ("I Wanna Be Sedated"), and the Phil Spector-produced *End of the Century* ("Rock 'n' Roll High School," "Do You Remember Rock 'n' Roll Radio?" "Chinese Rocks,") invariably did better in England than the U.S., with their remake of "Baby, I Love You," Spector's Ronettes classic, hitting the Top 10. Even 1985's wonderful anti-Reagan song, "Bonzo Goes to Bitburg," hit the Top 100 there.

"Chinese Rocks" first appeared on the album by the Heartbreakers and was covered by the Sex Pistols' notorious bassist Sid Vicious on his 1979 live solo album *Sid Sings*, miserably recorded in 1978 and released after he committed suicide while awaiting a murder rap. Vicious's work was a classic deconstruction of several eras of music as well his own work with the Sex Pistols. In addition, Vicious also took on Las Vegas (Frank Sinatra's "My Way," written by Paul Anka), the Brill Building (the Monkees' ("I'm Not Your) Stepping Stone," by Boyce and Hart), rockabilly (Eddie Cochran's "Something Else"), glam ("Born to Lose" by the Heartbreakers), and classic punk ("I Wanna Be Your Dog" and "Search and Destroy" by the Stooges).

By the time of Sid's death, the Sex Pistols' mission had been accomplished. With anti-anthems like "God Save the Queen" (their answer to the Beatles' impish "Her Majesty"), "Anarchy in the UK," "Holidays in the Sun," and "Pretty Vacant" (from 1977's *Never Mind the Bollocks Here's the Sex Pistols*), they'd said it all and spat it all in the face of the bloated music industry, to say nothing of Britain's decaying working-class culture. If the Damned had gotten there first, with their 1976 single "New Rose" presaging a new anti-studio, anti-virtuoso feeling in the air, the Sex Pistols brought it all crashing and burning to the surface within a few short, scathing, well-publicized years.

The Clash were just as uncompromising, recalling in their elemental rage no less a prophet of protest than Phil Ochs, who committed suicide only a year before their first album, *The Clash*, re-established the déclassé form to its prior relevance, with incendiary tracks like "London's Burning," "White Riot," and the reggae-inspired "Police and Thieves." *Give 'Em Enough Rope* followed with "Stay Free" and "All the Young Punks," their answer to David Bowie and the false front of glam. 1979's *London Calling* provided their credo, "Death or Glory."

Following the lead of Ramones, the Clash, and the Sex Pistols, punk rock stormed the barricades of Europe and America, giving rise to venom-fueled music unsurpassed in any era, as well as a return to the funky ethos of the independent 45. As early as 1974 on the Lower East Side of New York, Patti Smith, a rock 'n' roll poet with the voice of a Shangri-La, gave us "Piss Factory." Richard Hell's old band Television recorded "Little Johnny Jewel." In 1976, Hell and his new band the Voidoids released "Blank Generation." In Cleveland, Pere Ubu released "Final Solution" and then "Thirty Seconds over Tokyo." In Akron, Devo released "Monogloid." From Cleveland, the Dead Boys, produced by Genya Ravan, gave us "Sonic Reducer," from *Young and Loud and Snotty* in 1977. Punk finally reached California in 1978 with "Wasted" by Black Flag and "Adult Books" by X (with "We're Desperate" on the B side). In 1979, the Dead Kennedys released "California Über Alles."

England, however, was still storm central. Iggy Pop went to London to record *The Idiot* ("China Girl," "Sister Midnight") in 1977 and *Lust for Life* ("The Passenger") in 1978, produced by David Bowie, to whom many in the punk community claimed he'd sold his soul, while others said it presaged the post-punk era of electronica. "Orgasm Addict" by the Buzzcocks was a key 1977 single (followed by their era-defining "Ever Fallen in Love"). Their sometime touring partners Joy Division released the well-regarded *Unknown Pleasures* in 1979, preceded by the non-album single "Transmission." Then there was the thrilling agony of "Oh Bondage, Up Yours," by X-Ray Spex. As opposed to all the others, X-Ray Spex was led by a girl, teenager Poly Styrene. In 1978, Susan Dallion took a page out of the Yoko Ono playbook, moving over from the avant-garde art scene to become Siouxsie of Siouxsie and the Banshees. On their first album *The Scream*, the banshee label was particularly apt on their cover of "Helter Skelter." In the U.S. the album included their only UK Top 10 hit, the brilliant "Hong Kong Garden." 1978 was the year Kate Bush was discovered by Pink Floyd's David Gilmour, sounding a bit like Yoko Ono on her debut single "Wuthering Heights," from the musically bountiful *The Kick Inside* ("Man with the Child in His Eyes," "Them Heavy People"), which spent four weeks at Number One on the UK charts. The Slits, fronted by three females who appear clad mainly in mud on the album cover, toured with the Clash and were seen in *The Punk Rock Movie* before their first album *Cut* ("Typical Girls") arrived in 1979. More of a merger of Yoko and Nico, transplanted Detroit girl Lena Lovich made her debut with "Lucky Number," originally the B side of their Tommy James and the Shondells cover of "I Think We're Alone Now." ☞

Two of the most gifted artists of the punk period quickly shed that sometimes pejorative classification for the more civilized new wave label. The Police (Sting, Andy Summers, and Stewart Copeland) brought a reggae-lite touch to songs like "So Lonely," "Can't Stand Losing You," and "Roxanne," from 1978's *Outlandos d'Amour*. They had no trouble parlaying their virtuosity into eight Top 20 hits in the U.S. and ten Top 10 hits in the UK, including "Invisible Sun" (concerning the troubles in northern Ireland). Sting was even more successful as a solo artist, producing ten Top 20 hits on his own by the end of the century. Elvis Costello was the other prolific product of this era, arriving almost fully formed in 1977 with *My Aim Is True* ("Alison," "Less Than Zero," "Watching the Detectives"). With his Buddy Holly horn rims and a second coming of Presley swagger, Costello spewed songwriting angst and wordplay equal to Dylan in his heyday or John Lennon in his anti-Beatles prime, topping his debut effort with *This Year's Model*, in which he took on Bob Dylan doing Chuck Berry in "Pump It Up." Thereafter, he explored genres including country, R&B, chamber music, and classic pop, using the same mordant facility. All that was left to complete the circle was to write "Veronica" (1989) with Paul McCartney, which resulted in his biggest U.S. hit.

By the end of the decade, Ramones were already caught in their own limited formula, although that didn't prevent them from releasing fourteen albums, concluding with *Adios Amigos* in 1995. The Sex Pistols were gone. The Clash were releasing double and triple albums. They made the American Top 40 in 1980 with "Train in Vain (Stand by Me)," which caused everyone to doubt the band's remaining authenticity. Picking up the chalice, the Gang of Four released "Damaged Goods" in 1978, with "(Love Like) Anthrax" on the B side, containing the line "I feel like a beetle (Beatle?) on its back." Turning punk's depressive outlook into a genre in itself, the Cure released the controversial "Killing an Arab" in 1978. Bauhaus followed with the nine-minute epic "Bela Lugosi's Dead."

On May 18, 1980, the emotionally volatile fans of the genre received a kick in the teeth when Joy Division's driving force Ian Curtis committed suicide just before the band's first American tour. Their new song "Love Will Tear Us Apart" thus became his epitaph. One of the strange side effects of this suicide was that it prevented Martin Harnett, who produced both Joy Divison albums, from feeling up to taking on a new assignment. Thus, the U2 project fell into the hands of a young recording engineer named Steve Lillywhite, who'd recently played the glockenspiel on Siouxsie and the Banshees' hit single "Hong Kong Gardens," which was also hailed in the press for its guitar parts. He did the same on "I Will Follow," the leadoff track from U2's debut album *Boy*, which was released October 20, 1980. The song was an immediate underground hit. At last they'd found their Jimmy Page alternative sound!

But their euphoria was to be short lived, when on the evening of December 8 they learned, along with the rest of the worldwide musician and music fan community, that John Lennon had been shot in the back by a crazed lunatic outside of the Dakota Apartments in New York City. John's comeback single "(Just Like) Starting Over," would hit the top of the American charts three weeks later, informing the public of his new personal and musical maturity.

Clearly, a reappraisal was in the wind.

R.E.M., early 1980s.

12

THE AMERICAN ROOTS REVIVAL

American rock 'n' roll fans, especially those of a certain age, had been mourning the loss of Elvis Presley since August 16, 1977, when their musical icon was found dead in his bathroom. After his comeback with "Suspicious Minds" in 1969, he'd had twenty more Top 40 singles, including some of the greatest performances of his career, including "Rubberneckin'" (from his last movie, *A Change of Habit*), "Burnin' Love" (his last Top 10 hit), James Taylor's "Steamroller Blues," and Chuck Berry's "Promised Land." In addition, he ended a thirteen-year absence from the country Top 10 in 1970 with "There Goes My Everything." Between 1973 and 1975 he put four more songs into the upper reaches of the country charts: "I've Got a Thing About You, Baby," "Help Me," "It's Midnight," and "Hurt." In 1976, "Moody Blue" became his first country Number One since 1957. His next Number One wouldn't come until four days after he died, when "Way Down" was awarded the top spot for a week. A few months later, "My Way" was his first posthumous country Top 10. In 1978, "Unchained Melody" and "Are You Sincere" joined it. (The always tasteful Sid Vicious released his own version of "My Way" in 1978.) In 1979, Elvis's ghostly hold on the country charts continued with "There's a Honky Tonk Angel (Who Will Take Me Back In)." And in 1981, "Guitar Man" became his last country Number One, released a few weeks after John Lennon was murdered, peaking a week after Yoko Ono's "Walking on Thin Ice" began its ten-week run on the American singles chart.

Thus conjoined in sorrow, fans of two overlapping eras of memories and magic came together to stanch the drift of the anti-Elvis/ anti-Beatles forces in the world, to say nothing of the music industry. This would mean a return to the roots, epitomized by the early rock 'n' roll of Elvis and Gene Vincent, and harmony-based vocals attached to jangly guitars, epitomized by Buddy Holly, the Everly Brothers, the Beatles, Bob Dylan, and the Byrds. As an example of how outre the notion of the jangly guitar in a Top 40 single setting had become by 1977, when Gainesville, Florida's Tom Petty and the Heartbreakers released "American Girl," it was classified as alternative rock. And when transplanted Miami native Debbie Harry, enamored of the Shangri-Las, formed Blondie on the Lower East Side of Manhattan and released "X Offender" (produced by ex-Brill building hand and Angels producer Richard Gottehrer), it was called punk rock.

Outsized decibels reigned in America, whether at the disco, the converted hockey rink, or in the lungs of the angry punks within shouting distance of those two fat cat palaces. The best a former Beatles fan could hope for was the occasional melodic single from Cheap Trick. But their first few albums were produced by Tom Werman, who also produced Aerosmith, so such moments were usually buried under a professional gloss of studio noise. Early in 1980 they put out the EP *Found All the Parts*, containing their version of "Day Tripper." When they snagged Beatles producer George Martin for their next full length album *All Shook Up*, hopes were raised among the faithful. But the album was a commercial flop.

"My Sharona," by the perfectly packaged Los Angeles group the Knack, was a similar flashback to the power pop era, but the power petered out after "Good Girls Don't" and "Baby Talks Dirty" revealed them more as precursors to eighties heavy metal hair bands like Ratt and Poison.

Closer to the target was Shoes, a Zion, Illinois garage band (actually a living room band), that put out a brilliant independent power pop single in 1977 called "Tomorrow Night." It was re-released on their 1979 major label debut *Present Tense*. But further albums like *Tongue Twister* and *Boomerang* failed to capitalize on its underground success.

The first authentic taste of the changing zeitgeist was provided by Robert Gordon, a member of the punk rock group Tuff Darts, who appeared in the independent film *Unmade Beds* in 1976, which also featured Blondie's Debbie Harry. Gordon soon came to the attention of Blondie's producer Richard Gottehrer, who produced Gordon's first three albums, the first two of which featured rockabilly guitar legend Link Wray, with nods to giants of the forgotten form including "Summertime Blues" and "Twenty Flight Rock" (Eddie Cochran), "Boppin' the Blues" (Carl Perkins), "The Way I Walk" (Jack Scott), "A Red Cadillac and a Black Moustache" (Warren Smith), and "Red Hot" (Billy "The Kid" Emerson). Released right after the King's passing in 1977, "Red Hot" made the charts.

In 1980, the Blasters reaffirmed Gordon's basic sentiments with the classic "American Music" from the album of the same name, the first effort in the prolific output of the Alvin Brothers (Phil and Dave). Dave Alvin's 1987 solo album *Romeo's Escape* featured "The Fourth of July," which remains a classic of the genre. The Latin roots rock band Los Lobos broke through in 1984 with *How Will the Wolf Survive?*, more than fulfilling the promise of their first independent release in 1978, *Just Another Band from East L.A.*

Robert Gordon's next major impact on the new roots revival moved him closer to the jangly guitar camp with the 1981 album *Are You Gonna Be the One*, on which he covered three tunes by newcomer Marshall Crenshaw: "She's Not Mine Anymore," "But, But," and "Someday, Someway." Crenshaw's version of the latter song cracked the Top 40. But Crenshaw wasn't exactly a newcomer; in the late '70s he played John Lennon in the traveling Beatles-clone extravaganza *Beatlemania*. During the early part of his subsequent solo career, which started in 1982, he continued to play that up as well as down, until his quirky songwriting chops took over with tunes like "Cynical Girl," "Brand New Lover," "Whenever You're on My Mind" (covered by Ronnie Spector), and "You're My Favorite Waste of Time" (covered by Bette Midler). In 1987 he played Buddy Holly in the movie *La Bamba*, about the life of fallen rockabilly idol Ritchie Valens.

San Francisco's Flamin' Groovies had been waiting their whole career for this kind of music to return, having been dubbed hope-lessly retro ever since their 1969 debut album. After losing Roy Loney, one of their founding members, they moved to England, where they had the good fortune to meet fellow rockabilly fanatic Dave Edmunds, who had almost single-handedly kept the genre alive with albums like 1975's *Subtle As a Flying Mallet*, which con-tained covers of early rock classics like "Maybe," "Da Doo Ron Ron," "Baby, I Love You," and "A Shot of Rhythm and Blues." In 1976 Edmunds produced the Groovies' *Shake Some Action*, which contained covers of tunes by the Beatles ("Misery"), Chuck Berry ("Don't You Lie to Me"), and Larry Williams ("She Said Yeah"). In 1978, *The Flamin' Groovies Now* arrived, with covers of the Bea-tles ("There's a Place"), the Stones ("Paint It, Black," "Blue Turns to Grey"), and the Byrds ("I'll Feel a Whole Lot Better"). *Jumpin' in the Night*, issued in 1979, went even further, with covers of songs by Bob Dylan ("Absolutely Sweet Marie"), the Beatles ("Please Please Me"), and the Byrds ("5D," "Lady Friend," and "It Won't Be Wrong"). By this time Edmunds had returned to his own re-cording career, releasing *Get It* (1977), *Trax on Wax 4* (1978), and *Repeat When Necessary* (1979). With Nick Lowe, Edmunds formed Rockpile, which released *Seconds of Pleasure* (1980), sold with a bo-nus EP called *Dave Edmunds and Nick Lowe Sing the Everly Brothers*. This contained their versions of "Take a Message to Mary," "Cry-ing in the Rain," "When Will I Be Loved," and "Poor Jenny." In 1984, Edmunds took things one step further when he produced the Everly Brothers' comeback album *EB '84*, which contained the hit single "On the Wings of a Nightingale," written by Paul McCartney.

Taking a similar route as Flamin' Groovies, from the U.S. to Dave Edmunds' UK doorstep, were Stray Cats, whose name was taken from the 1974 rock flick *Stardust*. When they arrived in Lon-don in 1980, they caught the attention of every important band in town. Their first single "Runaway Boys," produced by Edmunds, hit the UK Top 10 in December, shortly after John Lennon was shot. Two months later they recorded "Rock This Town," which wasn't released in the U.S. until the fall of 1982. It finally reached the Top 10 in December. Neither their eponymous first album nor its follow-up *Gonna Ball* were released in the U.S., but the album that did eventually come out, *Built for Speed*, combined tracks from each, including "Rock This Town," "Stray Cat Strut," and the Eddie Cochran cover "Jeanie, Jeanie, Jeanie."

The Athens, Georgia-based B-52s mixed the hairstyles and attitudes of early sixties girl groups with a sensibility of the approaching electronic dance era. In 1978, their monster track "Rock Lobster" hit the UK Top 40, and along with "Cool," a 1979 single by four University of Georgia art students calling themselves Pylon, put Athens on the rock 'n' roll map. One of America's great college towns, Athens not only spawned a music scene but an entire sub-genre known as college rock. Not since the heyday of the baby boom elitism known as folk rock in the mid-sixties did a sound and feel take over a hungry sophisticated demographic, which had been enraged by the working class high school dropout mentality currently besieging their music. No group epitomized this genre better than R.E.M.

Learning their instruments at frat parties and rathskellers as they went along, Michael Stipe, Peter Buck, Mike Mills, and Bill Berry would soon become names almost as recognizable as John, Paul, George, and Ringo. Their first homegrown single "Radio Free Europe," was recorded at Mitch Easter's Drive-In Studios, which was literally that: a drive-in studio housed in Easter's family garage in Winston-Salem, North Carolina, a mere five-hour drive from Athens and an hour-and-a-half as the crow flies from Chapel Hill, another famous college town.

Easter had some credibility to back up his modest digs. His band the Sneakers had released *In the Red* in 1978, which aptly summed up the spirit of the coming anti-Zeppelin, anti-punk, and anti-Disco revolution. In 1972, Jonathan Richman recorded an homage to the Velvet Underground's "Sister Ray" called "Roadrunner," a glistening ode to being alone in a car in New England on a Saturday night. This thrilling single didn't see the light of day until the belated but timely release of *The Modern Lovers* in 1976. Although the Modern Lovers were influenced by the Velvet Underground,

Jonathan Richman was the mortal opposite of Lou Reed, a gentle soul trapped in the body of a compulsive performer. While "Roadrunner" has gained a number of punchy rock performances over the years (the Sex Pistols and Joan Jett and the Blackhearts among them), Richman pretty much disowned them, striking out in a different direction with a different band the same year the album came out, and one that was a lot closer to the late seventies' return to Americana.

Two of the Sneakers, Chris Stamey and Will Rigby, went on to form the dB's; in 1981 they released *Stands for Decibels*, with "Black and White" as the first single. Next came *Repercussion* in 1982, which included the single "Amplifier." Around the same time, Mitch Easter formed Let's Active, gaining a label deal by virtue of a perfect demo EP in 1983 called *Afoot*. That same year, he produced R.E.M.'s first album *Murmur* with Don Dixon, another local Chapel Hill hero, who had actually formed the band Arrogance in his University of North Carolina dorm room. Arrogance released a number of albums locally and had two shots at national recognition on major labels: *Rumors* in 1976 and *Suddenly* in 1980, but were unable to get over. He went on to produce albums by such stalwarts of the genre as Marshall Crenshaw, Richard Barone, Guadalcanal Diary, Tommy Keene, the Smithereens, Matthew Sweet, Marti Jones, and Beat Rodeo.

Included in *Murmur*, the defining track that launched a thousand college bands was the re-recorded version of "Radio Free Europe," which made the singles charts. The band and Don Dixon claim they still preferred the original 1981 version on law student Jonny Hibbert's Hib-Tone label, the first of four releases, which also included singles by the Throbs, Three Hits, and Harold Kelling (lead guitarist of the quirky artsy Atlanta-based group the Hampton Grease Band) before Hibbert closed up shop. Prior to their first full album, R.E.M. issued an EP called *Chronic Town*, from which came the shadowy but compelling video for "Wolves, Lower," which may have been seen by the band's few intrepid friends on *120 Minutes*, an alternative rock program on fledgling cable channel MTV.

Neither rap nor metal nor British new wave, jangly roots bands rarely showed up anywhere else on that rigidly programmed operation in the early eighties. But that suited their underground bent just fine. All around the country, the back-to-rock-and-roll movement was taking root. In Dayton, Ohio, Robert Pollard gave up the bar band circuit for his own twisted path, which centered around a string of limited run independent releases, one of which found its way into the record collection of R.E.M., immediately upping his profile immensely. In 1994, Pollard and friends finally quit their day jobs after *Bee Thousand* (Scat, 93) established them on the jangly college circuit.

In New Jersey, the Smithereens released their first two EPs, *Girls About Town* (1980) and *Beauty and Sadness* (1983), the latter particularly evoking the Beatles (if the Beatles, that is, had grown up listening to the Beatles, the Velvet Underground, and Ozzy Osbourne). Also from Jersey came the Feelies, which put the city of Hoboken on the musical map with *Crazy Rhythm* (1980), just in time to influence R.E.M. A highlight track was their cover of the Beatles' "Everybody's Got Something to Hide (Except Me and My Monkey)." Influenced by the Smithereens and the Feelies, Fountains of Wayne broke out of New Jersey as well, by way of Massachusetts a decade later, led by clever songwriter Adam Schlesinger, whose quirky output ("Stacy's Mom"), established the anti-Springsteen, anti-Bon Jovi sound. By this time the quirky/clever niche sometimes associated with the Beatles had been honed to a verbally manic pitch by the Brooklyn, New York-based duo They Might Be Giants ("Ana Ng"), the New Hope, Pennsylvania duo Ween ("Push Th' Little Daisies"), and the Toronto, Ontario duo of Ed Robertson and Steve Page, lead vocalists of Barenaked Ladies ("Be My Yoko Ono").

Three hours south of Toronto and a few years earlier in Jamestown, New York, near Buffalo, the members of the newly-christened 10,000 Maniacs added intense and dreamy seventeen-year-old lead singer Natalie Merchant to the lineup in 1982 and released the EP *Human Conflict Number Five*. *Secrets of the I Ching* followed in 1983, which included the popular track "My Mother the War," which also found its way onto 1985's *The Wishing Chair*. Their breakout album *In My Tribe* came in 1987, produced by Paul McCartney's almost-brother-in-law Peter Asher. Also in the area listening hard were Goo Goo Dolls, who followed the Replacements' model from punky sloppiness to Beatlesque balladry, culminating in their big 1995 hit "Name." Down in New York City, the experimental no wave band Sonic Youth, went in the opposite direction, putting out their 1982 debut album, the self-titled *Sonic Youth*. Their sound was relatively mellow and rootsy when compared to the atonal explorations and jangly noise that would follow, among them the epics "Teenage Riot" and "Silver Rocket," from the 1988 masterwork *Daydream Nation*.

In Milwaukee, Wisconsin, a stone's throw from Madison, home to the University of Wisconsin, and perhaps the most legendary of all college towns (especially during the late sixties), the Violent Femmes put out their own eponymous mixture of folk and punk anthems, an album containing their most famous tracks, many of which have gone on to a pop cultural life way beyond the scope of the band's original impact. "Blister in the Sun" was featured on an episode of the classic teen angst TV series *My So-Called Life*, in the semi-classic John Cusack-as-hit-man movie *Grosse Pointe Blank*, the 2007 coming-of-age film *Adventureland*, and referenced in John Green's coming-of-age novel *Paper Towns*. (It also appears in the movie *Rocket Science* along with "Kiss Off.") "Add It Up" is played by Ethan Hawke in the 1994 generation-co-defining movie *Reality Bites*. "Good Feeling" appears on an episode of the popular TV show *How I Met Your Mother* as Marshall and Lily's "song."

Further north on Interstate 35 in Minneapolis, just 200 miles south of Bob Dylan's birthplace in Hibbing, the Replacements carved out a space in the American rock dream of do-it-yourself glory following the new wave-influenced Suburbs to the local Twin-Tone label (which released Suburbs' first EP in 1978). Influenced by Dylan, Alex Chilton, and Kiss, the Replacements' first three releases, the 1981 album *Sorry Ma, Forgot to Take out the Trash*, the 1982 EP *Stink*, and the 1983 album *Hootenanny* represented their sloppy-drunk, let-it-all-hang-out-on-stage-Beatles-in-Hamburg phase. By the time *Let It Be* came out in 1984, Paul Westerberg had emerged as a songwriter who was not afraid to reveal his passionate jangly guitar side, in songs like "Sixteen Blue," "Unsatisfied," and "I Will Dare," which features a stellar rockabilly guitar solo by R.E.M.'s Peter Buck. Soul Asylum followed in their footsteps at TwinTone, along with the Jayhawks.

As usual, California brought the psychedelic influence to the party. While San Francisco had never truly recovered from the fall of the Summer of Love, down in L.A., a whole scene, dubbed "the Paisley Underground" by Michael Quercio (a member of one of its core bands, the Three O'Clock) emerged in 1981 as a love-and-peace-and-jangly-guitar alternative to bands like the Dead Kennedys, who were themselves an in-your-face punk rock alternative to the Beatles. The Three O'Clock's 1983 album *Sixteen Tambourines* featured the college hit "Jet Fighter." They put out five albums and called it a day after 1988's *Vermillion*.

The biggest band in the area, however, wasn't part of that scene. The Go-Gos were more like reincarnated surfer babes than flower children, an all-girl band with one foot in the pro and the other in the anti-Beatles camp, aligned with both the punk and power pop sounds along with a healthy commercial overlay of British new wave. Their first two singles, "Our Lips Are Sealed" (1981) and a re-recorded "We Got the Beat" (1982) were big hits, with the latter peaking at number two. The album *Beauty and the Beat* was number one for six weeks.

As opposed to the punky pop pretensions of the Go-Gos, the bands in the Paisley Underground were resolutely true to their name. The Velvet Underground-influenced Dream Syndicate was formed at the University of California Davis by Steve Wynn, whose seven-and-a-half-minute opus "The Days of Wine and Roses" (the title track of their first full-length album in 1983) was his high water mark. By this time Wynn had his own Down There label, on which he released the 1982 self-titled Green on Red EP. In 1985, Wynn and Green on Red vocalist Dan Stuart put out *The Lost Weekend* under the names Danny and Dusty, with great tracks like "Miracle Mile," "Song for the Dreamers," and a cover of Bob

Dylan's "Knockin' on Heaven's Door." The Long Ryders, featuring Sid Griffin on guitar and autoharp, harkened back on their 1983 release *10-5-60* to the Byrds and the Flying Burrito Brothers, and forward to the alt-country sound of Uncle Tupelo, Wilco, Son Volt, and the Jayhawks.

Easily the most successful of these bands was the all-girl Bangles, a foursome consisting of Susanna Hoffs and Vicki Peterson on guitars, Debbi Peterson on drums, and Annette Zilinskas on bass. Their first EP *Bangles* was released in 1983 along with the single "The Real World" (ten years prior to the debut of the MTV program of the same name) before the label folded and Zilinskas quit. She was replaced by Michael Steele, previously of the all-girl band the Runaways. Bangles' next release was *All Over the Place* (1984), which showed their Beatles influences on covers of songs by Emitt Rhodes ("Live") and Katrina and the Waves ("Going Down to Liverpool"). *Different Light*, released in 1986, further added to their tasteful credibility with songs written by Prince ("Manic Monday"), Alex Chilton ("September Gurls"), Jules Shear ("If She Knew What She Wants") and Akron, Ohio scene maker Liam Sternberg ("Walk Like an Egyptian"). "Manic Monday" hit Number Two on the charts in 1986 while "Walk Like an Egyptian" reached Number One.

The rootsy heartland sound was just about the only competition on the singles chart in the early eighties for the anti-rootsy sound coming from England. Previously, the mood of music fans was too dismally anti-Beatles to sustain such a movement after the 1975 success of "Born to Run" by New Jersey's premier heartland rocker Bruce Springsteen. But the Boss roared into a much more favorable climate in 1984 with an unprecedented run of seven Top 10 singles from his album *Born in the USA*. The way had already been greased by jangly old Tom Petty and the Heartbreakers, who hit with "Don't Do Me Like That" (1979), "Refugee" (1980), "The Waiting" (1981), and "You Got Lucky" (1982). Along with Springsteen came John Cougar Mellencamp, Indiana's hippest performer since James Dean, with I Need a Lover" (1979), "Ain't Even Done with the Night" (1981), "Hurts So Good" (1982), and "Pink Houses" (1983). Huey Lewis and the News, a bluesy bar band from San Francisco, hit it big in 1984 with "Heart and Soul," "I Want a New Drug," "The Heart of Rock and Roll," and "If This Is It," with all making the Top 10. Original retro rocker John Fogerty of Creedence Clearwater Revival had a successful comeback album in 1985 called *Centerfield* with "The Old Man Down the Road" hitting the Top 10. Even Alex Chilton came back in 1985 (after a five year album layoff), releasing the soulfully rootsy EP *Feudalist Tarts*, which contained "Thank You John," his tribute to John Lennon.

Two female singers who couldn't have been more different also emerged in 1984 to help define their gender for the remainder of the decade. Brooklyn's Cyndi Lauper evoked girl group history in her tormented voice on the album *She's So Unusual*, released in 1983, which transformed indie rock obscurities like Robert Hazard's "Girls Just Want to Have Fun" and Tom Gray's "Money Changes Everything" into empowering anthems. The album produced four hit records, including "Time After Time," which went to Number One. Lauper's quirky persona led her to an erratically eclectic career after that, including TV appearances on *Mad About You*, *The Simpsons*, *As the World Turns*, and *The Celebrity Apprentice* and in a Broadway production of *The Threepenny Opera*. A good friend of Yoko Ono's, Lauper was part of Lennon-Ono's Peace Choir along with Adam Ant, Bruce Hornsby, Sebastian Bach, Lenny Kravitz, Randy Newman, Iggy Pop, Bonnie Raitt, and Little Richard (who officiated at her wedding the same year). She performed Sean Lennon's rewrite of "Give Peace a Chance" as a response to the 1991 Gulf War.

The debut of Bay City, Michigan's future diva Madonna Ciccone, was only slightly less sensational, with three Top 20 hits in 1984: "Holiday," "Borderline," and "Lucky Star." But Madonna would remain the more consistent hit maker and female role model, adapting to the shifting sonic trends of the next two decades with the relentless smarts and intuition of a corporate barracuda.

This all-American logjam on the Top 40 not only led to a long-awaited renaissance of listening pleasure for fans of singles on the radio, but produced the unexpected side effect of fueling one of the last great underground rock scenes of the decade (if not the century) in and around the Roxbury, Massachusetts-based Fort Apache Studios. Barred from airspace by a new vinyl ceiling clogged with radio-friendly superstars (seven singles from one album eliminated a bunch of slots that might otherwise have gone to three or four different bands), they were thus free to thrash out their fledgling styles, lineups, and romantic entanglements leading to classic songs without undue interference from the bean counters. While this resulted in some endearing artifacts left behind for historians and local scene junkies to treasure, it also made for careers long on potential and short on beans: witness early scene makers the Lemonheads' prophetically-titled first EP *Laughing All the Way to the Cleaners*, released in 1986. Lead singer Evan Dando was among those who would fail the loudest, as pop star and potential new boyfriend, with 1992's "It's a Shame About Ray" being his surviving legacy.

By then, attention was being paid to the scene by virtue of 'Til Tuesday's 1985 Top 10 hit "Voices Carry," inspired by lead singer and songwriter Aimee Mann's tortured love life. Mann would eventually end her relationship with the band and resume a tortured career as a solo artist with *Whatever* in 1993, which featured songs called "I Should've Known," "Put Me on Top," "I Could Hurt You Now," and "I've Had It." Her next album was called *I'm with Stupid*.

In a neighborhood that was dangerous at night and iffy by day, the Fort Apache studios were right next door to a deserted ghetto schoolyard, looking out on a row of empty lots filled with abandoned cars; in other words, it was the perfect setting for uncompromising rock 'n' roll. Among the early discoveries of studio manager Gary Smith was Throwing Muses, a Rhode Island band featuring Kristen Hersh and her stepsister Tanya Donelly. Smith suggested the band move to Boston, which it did. At the Rat in Boston, Smith took an interest in a band opening for Throwing Muses called the Pixies (the brainchild of University of Massachusetts students Black Francis and Joey Santiago), which he would later produce. Throwing Muses self-titled debut came out in 1986 on the British 4AD label featuring nine songs by Hersh and one by Donelly. Their second album *House Tornado* was produced by Smith and engineered by Paul Kolderie at Fort Apache. This album featured nine songs by Hersh and two by Donelly. By this time Smith had delivered the legendary *The Purple Tape*, the Pixies' original demo tape, which was turned into the *Come on Pilgrim* EP. *Surfer Rosa* followed ("Bone Machine") and with *Doolittle*, they had arrived ("Debaser," "Here Comes Your Man," "Monkey Gone to Heaven"). At this point, original bass player Kim Deal started flirting with a side project called the Breeders, along with the disaffected Tanya Donelly. Their first release *Pod*, came out in 1990 on 4AD (which was also the Pixies' label), featuring eleven songs written or co-written by Kim Deal, one Deal-Donelly collaboration, and a cover of the Beatles' "Happiness Is a Warm Gun."

Smith produced *Earwig* (1989) and *Sunburn* (1990), the second and third albums by the Blake Babies, a band Juliana Hatfield started at the Berklee College of Music with John Strohm. Smith also produced Hatfield's first solo album, *Hey Babe* in 1992, on which she was joined by her once and future, on-again off-again love interest Evan Dando on backup vocals and guitar. Hatfield's commercial high point occurred when her track "Spin the Bottle" was used in the 1994 film *Reality Bites*, in which Dando made a cameo appearance.

One of the greatest single tracks to emerge from Fort Apache was "Freak Scene" by Dinosaur Jr. in 1988, which led off the band's third album *Bug*, a heartfelt summation of the indie rock ethos, both through its evocative, painful lyrics and its evocative, painful guitar part, a direct descendant of Neil Young's work on "Cinammon Girl." After completing this album, bass player Lou Barlow was drummed from the band, which left him plenty of time to focus on his side project Sebadoh, whose debut album, *The Freed Man*, containing 31 tracks, was released in 1989. His magnum opus, "Gimme Indie Rock," released in 1991, eventually led the band to sign with Sub Pop, whose first release, issued in 1992, was *Smash Your Head on the Punk Rock*. Barlow soon stumbled into a soundtrack assignment for the film *Kids*, from which "The Natural One" emerged as a fluke Top 30 single in 1995 under the name the Folk Implosion.

A s Lou Barlow recalled, "The Natural One" was recorded at Fort Apache. Summing up the indie rock experience almost as eloquently as his partner J. Mascis had, Barlow went on to explain, "I knew it would be okay, because it was Fort Apache. I knew I could walk in there cold and it would just work out. We recorded the song in six hours. How beautiful is that? For me, it was the creative thrill of it and also flying in the face of any kind of doing what you're told. Maybe even at that time at Fort Apache there was a certain feeling of the right way to do things. The right mike to put on this. The right guitar to play this part. But I always really disliked those notions.

"Nevertheless, to wind up with a hit single was totally weird," he said. "Once we had the success we obviously completely complicated the situation. I hate the feeling that when I walk into a situation, someone's expecting me to do something brilliant. When it comes to 'here we are following up our major label hit,' that sucks."

Ultimately, it would be the Seattle-based Sub Pop label that would define indie rock beginning in 1987, with single, EP, and album releases by a virtual who's who of the scuzzy, seat-of-the-pants genre. Starting with Green River's first EP *Dry as a Bone*, they had a franchise on the anti-Paisley sound of grunge with Soundgarden's first two EPs, *Screaming Life* (1987) and *Fopp* (1988), the 1988 combined Sonic Youth / Mudhoney single on which Sonic Youth covered Mudhoney's "Touch Me, I'm Sick" on one side and Mudhoney covered Sonic Youth's "Halloween" on the other. Mudhoney's first two albums, *Mudhoney* (1989) and *Every Good Boy Deserves Fudge* (1991) led to Nirvana's 1989 debut *Bleach*. The Sub Pop Record Club offered an array of singles to delight fans of the form, including "The Wagon" by Dinosaur Jr. (1990), Hole's second single, "Dicknail" (1991), Modest Mouse's first single "Broke" (1996), the White Stripes' Captain Beefheart trilogy, "Of the Special Things to Do," "China Pig," and "Ashtray Heart" (2000), "I Will Be Grateful for This Day, I Will Be Grateful for Each Day to Come" by Bright Eyes (2001), and Iron and Wine's "Call Your Boys" (2002). In 2001, they released the first of three albums by the

Shins, *Oh, Inverted World*, featuring the generational mood-defining "New Slang," which emerged in the soundtrack to the generational mood defining movie *Garden State*. That soundtrack also included Iron and Wine's cover of "Such Great Heights" from the 2003 album *Give Up* by the Postal Service, Death Cab for Cutie founder Ben Gibbard's side project.

The previous generation's mood-defining movie (sharing the marquee with *Reality Bites*) was 1997's *Good Will Hunting*, which featured six depressive songs by Portland, Oregon's anti-rock star Elliott Smith, including the haunting "Angeles" and the Oscar-nominated "Miss Misery." The film takes place in South Boston, within hailing distance of the original Roxbury location of Fort Apache Studios, which had long since relocated to the slightly more upscale city of Cambridge.

Completing a twenty-year cosmic circle, alt-country pioneer Steve Earle arrived by way of Nashville with *Guitar Town* in 1986, the first "New Dylan" since Steve Forbert in 1979. Deeper underground, R. Stevie Moore continued sending urgent recorded missives from his living room, as he had been doing since the late sixties. Indigo Girls emerged in 1987 from Atlanta's Emery University with *Strange Fire*, the first "New Simon and Garfunkel" since the originals last reunited with "My Little Town" in 1975. In 1990 Paisley Underground veteran Jason Falkner of the Three o'Clock formed Jellyfish and released *Bellybutton*, the first (and only) "New Badfinger," with two Badfinger covers and Paul McCartney's "Jet," which was available only in the UK. In 1991, Neutral Milk Hotel, the next R.E.M., emerged from Athens, Georgia, led by Jeff Mangum. Their album was released on Elephant 6, a label run by an outcast fraternity of musicians and bands that would include Apples in Stereo, Of Montreal, and the Olivia Tremor Control, as well as others that would break through later in the decade. Neutral Milk Hotel released *In the Aeroplane Over the Sea* in 1998 and broke up the following year before their work could be deemed an underground masterpiece (eventually with significant overground sales figures to back it up). In 1993, Gin Blossoms, out of Tempe, Arizona, channeled the great jangly sound of the Grass Roots with the hits "Hey Jealousy" and "Found out About You." In Los Ange-les a year later, Rivers Cuomo channeled Buddy Holly in Weezer's hit single and accompanying evocative video "Buddy Holly." (Like his father Bob, Jakob Dylan looked to the Byrds for his rock 'n' roll entry point with the Wallflowers' "6th Avenue Heartache").

In 1991, Tanya Donelly formed Belly, with the album *Star* arriv-ing in 1993, containing fourteen tracks written solely by her (with one co-write), including the hit single, "Feed the Tree."

But George Harrison almost had them all beat. In 1988, he per-formed the miraculous by creating the Traveling Wilburys, a super group to rival the Beatles, joined by Bob Dylan, Roy Orbison, Tom Petty, and Jeff Lynne. Their first single "Handle with Care" was a smash. There was talk of a tour, but Roy Orbison died of a heart attack before the second album, the perversely titled *The Traveling Wilburys, Volume Three* could be produced, and the Wilburys never traveled.

They might've been big.

Oasis, circa 1994.

13

THE BRITISH INVASIONS

In a way, the entire decade of the eighties could have been called "The Revenge of George Harrison."

Known as the quiet Beatle, the mysterious Beatles, the brooding Beatle, the sad Beatle, the spiritual Beatle, the sanctimonious Beatle, the hard-luck Beatle, and to John and Paul, the Baby Brother, George struck a particularly sympathetic note when he lost his wife to Eric Clapton in 1974. But it's safe to say that none of those sympathetic notes can be found on his landmark 1969 solo album *Electronic Sound*, on which George encounters the Moog synthesizer, changing music forever.

As he unconsciously did a year later with "My Sweet Lord," George co-opted an entire tune on this album from something he'd heard before. "No Time or Space," which consumed all of Side Two, was derived from a demonstration lesson given to him by his original Moog guru Bernie Krause, who was credited as an "assistant" on the album but not given any credit at all on the CD reissue. (For an additional cosmic joke, the CD reversed the two song titles on the original LP.)

Paralleling the course taken by Ronnie Mack, author of "He's So Fine," (the song "My Sweet Lord" was based on), Krause took his former student to court. But lost in the legal shuffle was George's embracing of the synthesizer, which first showed up on four songs from *Abbey Road*, "Because," "Here Comes the Sun," "I Want You (She's so Heavy)," and "Maxwell's Silver Hammer." Like all of the Beatles' various sonic inventions, the synthesizer soon became an essential thread in the fabric not only of psychedelic music, but progressive rock, fusion, funk, disco, and the British Invasion of the 1980s.

Krause and his partner Paul Beaver introduced the first Moog to the hipsterati at the Monterey International Pop Festival in 1967. Shortly after, Krause hooked one up for Ray Manzarek of the Doors to use on the title track for *Strange Days*. Mick Jagger also fiddled around with a Moog on the Stones' *Their Satanic Majesties Request*. Beaver contributed "Synthesthesia" to the soundtrack of the Peter Fonda / Jack Nicholson pre-*Easy Rider* psychedelic epic *The Trip* and also played on "Goin' Back," "Natural Harmony," and "Space Odyssey" from *The Notorious Byrd Brothers*. His Moog work shows up on "Star Collector" and "Daily Nightly" from the Monkees' *Pisces, Aquarius, Capricorn & Jones Ltd*. Krause also appeared on the Electric Flag's debut album and Simon and Garfunkel's *Bookends* ("Save the Life of My Child"). After showing George the ropes, Krause was hired to work his magic on Jackie Lomax's 1969 Apple debut *Is This What You Want?*

In 1968, composer Walter Carlos (still four years away from becoming Wendy) showcased the Moog in the platinum-selling *Switched-on Bach*, influencing long-haired rock musicians like Keith Emerson and Rick Wakeman to add it into their repertoire, forming the progressive basis for ELP and Yes. Jan Hammer and John McLaughlin incorporated it into the Mahavishnu Orchestra's trailblazing *Inner Mounting Flame*, giving rise to the much scoffed at fusion genre. In 1969 *The Minotaur* by Dick Hyman and His Electric Eclectics brought a taste of space age pop to the mix. Gershon Kingsley's 1969 album *Music to Moog By* featured covers of "Nowhere Man" and "Paperback Writer." In 1972, Stan Free, Kingsley's partner in the First Moog Quartet, covered Kingsley's "Popcorn" under the name Hot Butter, which became a huge international hit. From 1972 to 1976, Stevie Wonder took up the chalice in five albums, from *Music of My Mind* through *Songs in the Key of Life*. In 1974 the future of electronic music virtually got its template from Ralf Hütter and Florian Schneider, the masterminds behind Kraftwerk, whose *Autobahn* was a blockbuster, with an edited version of the title track becoming a hit single in the U.S. as well as in England. Bernie Worrell brought the synth to Parliament's 1977 hit "Flashlight," and Giorgio Morodor translated it to the disco crowd in Donna Summer's megahits "Love to Love You Baby" and "I Feel Love."

In the heyday of punk, it was time for the Moog to be reconsidered. In Akron, Ohio, the geek rock band Devo put out *Q: Are We Not Men? A: We Are Devo!* with the anti-anthemic "Jocko Homo" and a unique approach to "(I Can't Get No) Satisfaction." But it wasn't until 1980's *Freedom of Choice* ("Whip It") that synthesizers became a prominent part of their act. In England, Gary Numan and Tubeway Army put out the album *Replicas* early in 1979, with the hit UK single "Are Friends Electric?" Numan followed with the solo album *The Pleasure Principle* and his only U.S. hit, "Cars." Both were dominated by the mini-Moog, as were Numan's five other Top 10 UK singles from 1979 to 1982: "Complex," "We Are Glass," "I Die: You Die," "She's Got Claws," and "We Take Mystery (to Bed)." The sound of the latest invasion had arrived.

This was far different from the sound of the first British Invasion, which was, of course, much more directly Merseyesque. Owing to the lack of American rock bands ready to fill the void, Liverpool and its Mersey River environs became a viable scene in 1964 and the model for future record label gold rushes into San Francisco; Akron, Ohio; Athens, Georgia; and Seattle, Washington. Groups managed by Brian Epstein made out like cheap high school sluts on the coattails of the Beatles. The first of these, Gerry and the Pacemakers, gladly recorded "How Do You Do It," the song the Beatles turned down during their initial meeting with George Martin, spending three weeks at Number One in England in 1963 and one week at Number 9 in the U.S. a year later. Their next tune (also a Number One) was "I Like It," lifted from the repertoire of the Dave Clark Five. Their place in Merseybeat history was secured forever with the nostalgic "Ferry Cross the Mersey" from the movie of the same name. Billy J. Kramer and the Dakotas benefitted from the Brian connection by snagging four future Top 10 singles written by Lennon and McCartney: "Do You Want to Know a Secret" (which was a hit in the UK only), "Bad to Me," "I'll Keep You Satisfied," and "From a Window." Cilla Black, Brian's only female client, launched her career with Lennon and McCartney's "Love of the Loved." She went on to become a huge star in England with eleven Top 10 hits, including "Anyone Who Had a Heart" and "You're My World," which was her biggest hit in the U.S., peaking at Number 26. The jangly Mersey Sound's first American iteration came via the Cyrkle (also managed by Epstein), which had a couple of singles written for them, respectively, by Paul Simon and the Seekers' Bruce Woodley: "Red Rubber Ball" (a 1966 hit, originally a flop for the Seekers) and "I Wish You Could Be Here" (a 1967 flop).

Since England itself would only rank twenty-eighth in size among American states (after Arkansas and before Alabama, two slots larger than New York), the invasion quickly spread to the UK's furthest reaches, encompassing the sound of groups that had been influenced by the concurrent blues revival. When including the Beatles, the acts of the initial British Invasion accounted for twenty percent of the year's Top 40 records (60 out of 302 singles). These included lite-rock Merseyites (Herman's Hermits and the Dave Clark Five), pop rock entities (the Honeycombs and the Bachelors), folkie groups (the Hollies, the Searchers, the Zombies, Peter and Gordon, and Chad and Jeremy), and pop chanteuses (Dusty Springfield, Petula Clark, and Sandie Shaw). These lighter weight groups stood alongside harder rocking bands like the Rolling Stones, the Animals, the Kinks, the Nashville Teens, and Manfred Mann. Not to be forgotten was Top 40 mainstay Cliff Richard, who'd first visited the chart shores in 1959, and Beatles label mate and quasi-yodeler Frank Ifield, who peaked in 1963 with "I Remember You." Further down the charts, debut singles could be found by such stellar British artists as the Swinging Bluejeans, with the local Liverpool favorite "Hippy Hippy Shake," plucky belter Lulu, the folkie Overlanders, Brian Poole and the Tremeloes (the group Decca signed after turning down the Beatles), and Scott English, an American singer-songwriter based (fittingly enough) in London. (English later wrote a song called "Brandy" that Clive Davis would retitle and Barry Manilow would turn into the hit "Mandy.")

In 1965 British acts did even better, accounting for twenty-five percent of the American Top 40, with the Who, the Yardbirds,

Donovan, the Troggs, Them (from Belfast, featuring Van Morrison), the Spencer Davis Group (featuring Stevie Winwood), Tom Jones (from Wales), the Walker Brothers, Freddie and the Dreamers, Wayne Fontana and the Mindbenders, Roy Head, Jonathan King, the Fortunes, the Moody Blues, Shirley Bassey, the Silkie, Georgie Fame, Matt Monro, Ian Whitcomb, and future Monkee Davy Jones joining the party.

By this time enough American bands had come into existence to restore a bit of parity, although the extremely Beatlesque Bee Gees would soon be on their way from Australia, Rod Stewart would come along with Jeff Beck Group, and Eric Clapton's new power trio Cream, featuring Ginger Baker on drums and Jack Bruce on bass, bringing the two groups an advanced level of virtuosity to the mix.

While the first British Invasion may have been a two-to-four-year frenzy of a scene being squeezed to its last drop, the presence of British singers and bands on the American charts was no passing fad. It's impossible to rewrite history, but had the Beatles not crossed over; had they thrived solely in England as did Mud or the Status Quo, it is quite possible that the market for English sounds in America after 1964 would have petered out. Instead, starting with 1964, there wouldn't be a year where at least one British single didn't top the American charts until 1996! Only nine songs made Number One that year. (The tenth biggest song of the year was by Welsh lass Donna Lewis.) The next year more than made up for this when Elton John's worldwide smash remake of "Candle in the Wind" (to mourn the passing of Princess Diana) became the top song of the year and the Spice Girls (and their requisite Spicemania) became a Beatlesque fad.

The impact of the Beatles-led invasion cannot be understated. Especially on the FM dial. This is where Led Zeppelin reigned for a decade as the demigods of heavy metal along with Black Sabbath, Deep Purple, and Motorhead, until they were edged off the mountaintop by a second wave of British heavy metal, including Judas Priest, Iron Maiden, and Def Leppard. FM was the delivery system that propelled Pink Floyd's *The Dark Side of the Moon* to a record-setting three generations on the album charts. Here were stations that welcomed in all its eight-minute song glory the genre known as progressive rock, featuring Yes, Genesis, Emerson, Lake and Palmer, King Crimson, Jethro Tull, the Alan Parsons Project, and Queen. It is where the hard rock of Brit bands like Bad Company, Free, UFO, Peter Frampton, Ritchie Blackmore's Rainbow, and Paul McCartney's Wings were considered as American as Mom's Apple Pie (an American rock band known primarily for a salacious album cover). Like white acts mistaken for black on the doo-wop circuit of the fifties, it's possible the few American rock bands that infiltrated the FM playlists of the 1970s were initially thought of as being British, although in actuality they came from New England (Aerosmith), New York (Blue Oyster Cult and Mountain), and the Midwest (Styx and Grand Funk Railroad). Some, like Fleetwood Mac and Foreigner, were actually half-British. The Jimi Hendrix Experience was formed, fed, and nurtured in England, only to be shipped back to the states as a new entity in much the same way the Beatles remodeled rock 'n' roll.

Even as anti-Beatlemania threatened to obliterate their jangly legend in the mid-seventies (mainly courtesy of punk rock, a mostly British rage-infused genre), there was always at least one band left standing to keep the flame a flicker. In the U.S., the Knack and Cheap Trick were dubbed power pop for their Beatlesque leanings. In the UK, Jeff Lynne made it his self-professed mission to top "Strawberry Fields Forever" after joining the Move in 1970 and changing his group's name to the Electric Light Orchestra. ELO's second UK hit was a cover of Chuck Berry's "Roll Over Beethoven" (which the Beatles also covered), which almost cracked the U.S. Top 40. They went on to twelve Top 10 hits in the UK from 1972 to 1979 (five in the U.S.), nearly keeping the candle glowing all by their lonesome.

But ELO was not alone in keeping the candle glowing, as they were joined in their belief in the jangly essence of Beatlemania in 1973 by the obscure newspaper *Liverpool Echo*, which was also the name of a band featuring Martin Briley. (Briley would re-emerge in 1983 with the Top 40 hit "The Salt in My Tears.") Much more successful was 10cc, a group rife with first invasion roots. They were formed in 1972 by Eric Stewart and Graham Gouldman, who had been in the Mindbenders. Gouldman had written hits for Herman's Hermits and the Hollies. Kevin Godley and Lol Creme, in the tradition of John Lennon, were art students with a caustic edge. Although they were rejected by Apple, they would have been perfect in the label's declining days. Their songs were a mixture of high art and low comedy; an underground sensibility with a commercial foundation. The studio they worked out of and co-owned was named Strawberry Studios after "Strawberry Fields Forever." As a group they were behind the ghosting of several hits for New York's bubblegum impresarios Kazenetz & Katz, providing music, lyrics, voices, and arrangements for the Ohio Express and Crazy Elephant. But their biggest breakthrough was the transatlantic smash "I'm Not in Love," which in some circles is considered the best pop record of all time. More importantly, it earned them a big record company advance. Godley and Creme left in 1976 to pursue other options, among them the new field of music video direction, which was about to become an art form in the eighties. The two directed some of the best of the early MTV crop, including George Harrison's "When We Was Fab," Duran Duran's "Girls on Film," and the Peter Gabriel / Kate Bush duet "Don't Give Up." In 1992, 10cc reunited for an album called *Meanwhile*, which featured "Don't Break the Promises," co-authored by Stewart, Gouldman, and a promising young fellow named Paul McCartney.

By this time "Rollermania" was upon the land (in full Tartan regalia), the biggest teen craze in England since the Beatles for a new generation of thirteen year old girls too young to have experienced the real thing. The Bay City Rollers were from Edinburgh, Scotland, just 200 miles up the road from Liverpool. In their early albums they covered the Ronettes' "Be My Baby" and the Four Seasons' "Bye, Bye, Baby," the latter becoming the Number One song in the UK in 1975. To echo the reasoning of Capitol Records in the early sixties, this was just enough to convince Arista Records' Clive Davis to take a chance on them in America. In October 1975, Davis had the band play their 1973 flop "Saturday Night" on a live feed for television's *Saturday Night Live with Howard Cosell*, an ill-fated attempt by the garrulous sportswriter to morph into Ed Sullivan. The song's appearance had its Sullivanian effect nonetheless, reaching the top of the U.S. charts during the first week of January 1976. The Bay City Rollers would have six more Top 40 hits in the U.S. in the next couple of years, before lapsing, as the Beatles had before them, into drug revelations and withering lawsuits.

With so much Beatlemania in the air, naturally someone had to emerge to correct it. This was the mission of *All You Need Is Cash*, a 1978 TV "mockumentary" on the life and times of the Rutles, produced by Monty Python's Eric Idle and *Saturday Night Live*'s Lorne Michaels. After bombing in the U.S. on NBC, it achieved due recognition by the more discerning British TV audience a week later. An outgrowth of an episode of the Idle-Innes 1975–76 series *Rutland Weekend Television* (Britain's version of the droll Canadian sketch show *SCTV*), the Rutles lovingly spoofed every aspect of the Beatles legend, and included fourteen songs written by Innes, which were featured on the soundtrack album. (Six more were added to the CD reissue.) The cameos that graced *All You Need Is Cash* represented a highlight reel of British and American comedic talent, including Monty Python's Michael Palin and original *Saturday Night Live* cast members John Belushi, Dan Aykroyd, Gilda Radner, and Bill Murray. SNL writer/performers Al Franken and Tom Davis were also on hand, as well as frequent host Paul Simon. Mick Jagger and then wife Bianca didn't want to miss out on the fun, while fellow Stone Ronnie Wood played a Hell's Angel. Noted Liverpool performance poet Roger McGough, (who'd been in the Scaffold with Paul McCartney's brother Mike McGear) played himself. Of all the Beatles, the one who appreciated the joke most was, the droll Beatle himself, George Harrison, who played a TV newscaster presiding over the ransacking of the station, much as all four Beatles presided over the public demise of Apple Records.

But in the next decade, an even better revenge was in store for Harrison.

By then, the whimsically progressive Beatlesque group Supertramp had broken through with *Breakfast in America* ("The Logical

Song"). The new songwriting team of Chris Difford and Glenn Tilbrook from Squeeze was being hailed as the best since Lennon and McCartney (or at least since John and Taupin), with albums like 1979's *Cool for Cats* ("Cool for Cats," "Up the Junction"), 1980's *Argybargy* ("Pulling Mussels [from the Shell]," "Another Nail in My Heart," If I Didn't Love You"), 1981's *East Side Story* ("Tempted"), and 1982's *Sweets from a Stranger* ("Black Coffee in Bed"), after which they broke up. Originally a progressive punk band, the Soft Boys (*A Can of Bees*) eventually produced one genuinely Lennonesque artist, Robyn Hitchcock, who covered John Lennon's "Cold Turkey" on that album and would go on to underground fame with tracks like "Madonna of the Wasps" (1989) and "So You Think You're in Love" (1991). But by far the most Beatlesque new band of the era was XTC, led by the obsessive, stage-stricken Andy Partridge. Releasing their first full album, the punk-flavored *White Music* in 1978, XTC gradually evolved so that by 1986 they had become a full-service, lush, psychedelic-era Beatles-art-rock-throwback with *Skylarking*, featuring Partridge doing John Lennon on the surprise hit single "Dear God." (originally the B side of Colin Moulding's exceptionally Beatlesque "Grass.") "Summer's Cauldron" and "Earn Enough for Us" are other standouts from the album, which was produced by noted Beatles connoisseur Todd Rundgren.

Nineteen-eighty-six was the peak year for the biggest British invasion of America since the mid-sixties, with British acts accounting for a whopping thirty-four percent of the year's Top 40 (68 out of 211 singles), including nine Number One songs. Even the Beatles returned to the charts in 1986 with a reissue of "Twist and Shout," which lapsed at Number 23.

Although British acts were a consistent feature on American playlists during the 1970s, the latest invasion began as a trickle soon after John Lennon was shot on December 8, 1980. Latent Beatle fans around the world reacted to his death, which occurred one month after his much-anticipated comeback single, "(Just Like) Starting Over," was released. In England the song had already slipped to Number 21 only to leap to Number One on December 20. One week after that, it was Number One in America. In 1981,

"Woman," another single from the album, replaced it on the U.S. Top 10, joined a few months later by George Harrison's tribute, "All Those Years Ago." Ringo's anguished "Wrack My Brain," also written by George, made the Top 40.

In 1982, "Ebony and Ivory," Paul's semi-detached duet with Stevie Wonder from *Tug of War*, topped the chart. Buried in the album was Paul's poignant tribute to his former partner, "Here Today."

But the real clue to the future was to be found in several other hits. Beginning with Gary Numan's 1980 song "Cars," synth-based songs started to cross the Atlantic, the choicest among them being "Don't You Want Me" by Human League, "I Ran" by A Flock of Seagulls, "Tainted Love" by Soft Cell, and "Stand or Fall" by the Fixx. Aided by video exposure over MTV, George's long-envisioned synth revolution was upon us. In 1983, the British presence on the Top 40 doubled. While McCartney put a pair of singles with his business partner Michael Jackson on the top of the charts ("Say Say Say" reaching Number One; "The Girl Is Mine" making it to Number Two), American music fans not especially attuned to activities across the pond were introduced to a slew of acts that would define the sound of modern rock for the rest of the decade; among them Eurythmics, Culture Club, Duran Duran, Thomas Dolby, the Pretenders, Spandau Ballet, Madness, Kajagoogoo, Naked Eyes, Adam Ant, Wham, Ultravox, Tears for Fears, Heaven 17, Haysi Fantaysi, Bananarama, ABC, the Thompson Twins, the Psychedelic Furs, Dexy's Midnight Runners, and just for good measure, U2.

Not a bad year.

The singles results for 1984 were even more impressive, with England taking care of thirty percent of the Top 40, mainly with acts that debuted in 1983, which were joined by Frankie Goes to Hollywood and the Style Council. John Lennon's "Nobody Told Me," from the posthumous *Milk and Honey* album, hit the Top Five. In the UK, Julian Lennon had a Top 10 hit with "Too Late for Goodbyes," which peaked in America at the beginning of 1985, a few months after "Valotte." The new year maintained the same level of dominance for British acts, with Depeche Mode and Bronski Beat added to the populace along with headier creations from the Smiths, Prefab Sprout, and the Housemartins (which spun off into the Beautiful South in 1990). In 1986 Paul McCartney had his last Top 10 hit of the century, the theme from the movie *Spies Like Us*. But it was also a banner year for Ozzy Osbourne, making his solo debut with "Shot in the Dark," and John and Andy Taylor, taking a break from Duran Duran (John with "I Do What I Do," the theme for the movie *9 1/2 Weeks*, and Andy with "Take It Easy"). Mike Rutherford (formerly of Genesis) returned with Mike and the Mechanics. Steve Hackett (also from Genesis) put together GTR with Steve Howe (from Yes). The Art of Noise aligned with both Duane Eddy (to recreate "Peter Gunn") and the computer-generated Max Headroom (to create "Paranoimia"). The year's most auspicious debuts were by the Pet Shop Boys ("West End Girls") and Simply Red ("Holding Back the Years"). The year's least auspicious debut was by the Cure, whose "In Between Days (Without You)" spent one week at Number 99. But it was a start.

By 1987, the Invasion was on the wane, although two of the most Beatlesque groups were established, New Zealand's Crowded House ("Don't Dream It's Over" and "Something So Strong") and Karl Wallinger's World Party ("Ship of Fools"). George Harrison also had a good year, with his cover of James Ray's "Got My Mind Set on You" becoming his first Number One since 1973. Feeling the tickle of competition, Paul McCartney started collaborating with the closest person to John Lennon he could find, Elvis Costello. Their maiden effort was "Back on My Feet," which was used as the B side of "Once Upon a Long Ago," Paul's last Top 10 hit in the UK (although unreleased in the U.S.). Elvis wound up co-writing four songs for Paul's 1989 album *Flowers in the Dirt:* "You Want Her Too," "That Day Is Done," "Don't Be Careless Love," and "My Brave Face" (Paul's last appearance on the Top 40). To return the favor, McCartney co-wrote two songs for Costello's 1989 album *Spike*, "Pads, Paws and Claws" and "Veronica," the latter becoming Elvis's biggest U.S. hit.

George had an even better year in 1988. The video for his nostalgic "When We Was Fab," directed by Godley and Creme, got six nominations at the MTV Video Music Awards and featured a Hall of Fame lineup of cameos, including Ringo Starr, Elton John, Paul Simon, co-writer Jeff Lynne, Gary Wright, drummer-for-the-stars Ray Cooper, ex-Beatles publicist Derek Taylor, and ex-Beatles road manager Neil Aspinall. Later that year, George formed the Traveling Wilburys, a super group to end all super groups, with two of his idols (Roy Orbison and Bob Dylan), his main acolyte (Jeff Lynne), and Dylan's main acolyte (Tom Petty). Getting together over dinner in Malibu to record a B side for Harrison's single "This Is Love," the guys came up with "Handle with Care," which was not only strong enough to be released as a single on its own, but it inspired them to hang out long enough to complete a pseudonymous album over nine days in May. *Traveling Wilburys, Vol. 1* went to Number 3 on the U.S. album chart and sold three million copies.

Take that, Derek & the Dominos.

The last important mini-British Invasion took place from 1995 through 1997, which featured Beatles-influenced Brit-pop bands (the Stone Roses, Suede, Take That, Radiohead, Elastica, Pulp, Supergrass, Blur, Everything but the Girl, and Oasis), precious dream pop purveyors (Belle and Sebastian, the Sundays, the Cranberries, the Corrs, the Las, the Boo Radleys, and Mazzy Star), harder rockers (Bush, Sponge and P. J. Harvey), electronica stalwarts (the Chemical Brothers, Prodigy, and White Town), acid jazz (Jamiroquai's "Virtual Insanity"), and the anarchic world beat of Chumbawamba ("Tubthumping").

This set the stage for the Spice Girls: Victoria, Melanie B., Emma, Melanie C., and Geri, Britain's answer to New England's New Kids on the Block, who had six Top 10 hits in 1989. This led to another girl group explosion to rival that of the late 1950s and early sixties, including Boyzone, Eden's Crush, Dream, B'Witched, All Saints, SWV, TLC, Destiny's Child (Beyonce's proving ground) and culminating with the manufacture of the Pussycat Dolls. This was then answered by a boy band revival of the New Kids sound featuring Hanson, the Backstreet Boys, 'N Sync, Five, LFO, O-Town, 98 Degrees, solo comebacks by old New Kids Jordan Knight and Joey McIntyre, and culminating with the cloning of the Jonas Brothers.

The final crowning touch in all this end-of-the-century synthmania-turned Beatlemania was the unearthed and unfinished John Lennon demos donated by Yoko Ono to the Fab Three to help them promote their upcoming *Anthology* project, consisting of a documentary, three double albums and a book. Released in 1996, "Free as a Bird" and "Real Love" were the last official "Beatles" recordings and the first since "The Long and Winding Road" in 1970. They were both quite successful, as was the *Anthology* project.

But not quite as successful as Oasis, which broke from the pack in 1995 with their definitively Beatlesque second album *(What's the Story) Morning Glory*, which became the third best-selling album in UK history, behind a greatest hits collection by Queen and the one and only *Sgt. Pepper's Lonely Hearts Club Band*. Among its choice singles ("Don't Look Back in Anger," "Some Might Say," "Champagne Supernova," "Roll with It") is a track called "Wonderwall," an obvious tribute to George Harrison's *Wonderwall Music* from 1968.

Take that, Big Brothers.

The Beatles, circa 1969.

14

HERE TODAY

Since the death of George Harrison in 2001, the Beatles' lore, legend, and legacy has been carried forward (as it probably should be), by Paul McCartney, who has released six albums in the new millennium, including two live collections and a classical work. During the same period, his first, last, and only remaining competition for generational supremacy, Bob Dylan, has put out seven, including two weird movie soundtrack compilations (*Masked and Anonymous* and *I'm Not There*) and a Christmas album. The Beatles' catalog has withstood a few soundtrack compilations as well, including *I Am Sam* (2002), *Across the Universe* (2007), and *Nowhere Boy* (2010).

I Am Sam starred Sean Penn, Dakota Fanning, and Michelle Pfeiffer in the sentimental story of a developmentally-challenged man trying to raise his young daughter Lucy by himself. The soundtrack, however, is a challenging mix of Beatle covers by an all-star contemporary cast, including Aimee Mann and Michael Penn ("The Two of Us"), Sarah McLachlan ("Blackbird"), the Wallflowers ("I'm Looking through You"), Sheryl Crow ("Mother Nature's Son"), the Black Crowes ("Lucy in the Sky with Diamonds"), Eddie Vedder ("You've Got to Hide Your Love Away"), Ben Folds ("Golden Slumbers"), Ben Harper ("Strawberry Fields Forever"), Paul Westerberg ("Nowhere Man"), Nick Cave ("Let It Be"), and Rufus Wainwright ("Across the Universe").

"Across the Universe" lends its name to a movie in which various Beatles songs conspire to tell the story of the psychedelic sixties, which is in part the story of the Beatles. Here, most of the Beatle covers are done by the actors, although not necessarily to their best advantage. The performances by Bono on "I Am the Walrus" and "Lucy in the Sky with Diamonds" are not among his choicest moments either. Joe Cocker comes off best, in a self-parodying version of "Come Together."

Nowhere Boy is the story of a young John Lennon, focusing on the early rock 'n' roll that informed his coming of age in the late fifties. As a sampler of the period, it's a good one, including "Twenty Flight Rock" (Eddie Cochran), "Hound Dog" (Big Mama Thornton), "Shake, Rattle and Roll" (Elvis Presley), "Wild One" (Jerry Lee Lewis), "Be Bop a Lula" (Gene Vincent), and "Hard Headed Woman" (Wanda Jackson). Disc One concludes with John Lennon singing "Mother." Disc Two includes "Roll Over Beethoven" (Chuck Berry), "Peggy Sue" (Buddy Holly), "Rip It Up" (Little Richard), "Baby, Let's Play House (Elvis Presley), "Rock Around the Clock" (Bill Haley and His Comets), "Money" (Barrett Strong), "Ain't That a Shame" (Fats Domino), and the find of the package, "Brand New Cadillac" by Vince Taylor and His Playboys.

Perhaps the weirdest-grandest-tribute-exploitation of Beatles material was the 2006 show simply called *Love*, conceived and presented by the acrobatic dance troupe Cirque du Soleil at the Mirage Hotel in Las Vegas. Blessed by George Harrison in 2000, it took three years to gain the other necessary signatures from Paul, Ringo, and the surviving widows of John and George. Musically directed by George Martin and his son Giles, the biographical storyline samples and re-orchestrates 130 Beatle songs into twenty-eight discrete pieces in a free floating biographical collage. (In 2006 noted experimental choreographer Twyla Tharp had a similar crack at Dylan's catalog in the Broadway flop *The Times They Are-a Changin'*.)

For fans of a less elaborate yet more musically satisfying Beatles homage, the all-star tribute band the Fab Faux, featuring Will Lee and Jimmy Vivino, is recommended. Their always creative and virtuosic approach to the material has gained them the reputation as being the best of the approximately infinite number of working Beatles tribute bands.

Although there hasn't been another official British Invasion on the order of the one led by Oasis in the decade of the single digits, England's biggest contribution recently seems to be in the realm of soulful chanteuse Lisa Stansfield, the first white female ever to top the British R&B charts (with "All Around the World" in 1990). Since then, Beth Orton has broken through on the coffee house circuit, Dido has charmed the dancehalls, Joss Stone has displayed her massive blues chops, the late Amy Winehouse took home a boatload of Grammys, and biracial belter Leona Lewis won the *X Factor* (the British version of *American Idol*) and translated it into American success). They were followed by Lily Allen, Adele, Duffy, and Florence and the Machine.

Male solo artists and bands in the UK have fared much worse, with the most popular among them failing to cross over with any sort of impact, as with Ireland's Westlife, which hit Number One in the UK with its first seven singles, only one of which made the U.S. charts. The top UK male artist of the nineties, Take That veteran Robbie Williams, is Cliff Richard all over again; big in England, and an afterthought in the U.S. James Blunt had an international best-seller with "You're Beautiful" in 2006, but this seems so far to have been a one-shot. Alternative acts like Badly Drawn Boy, Travis, and Arctic Monkeys haven't traveled especially well. Arctic Monkeys' last three albums have been hits, but they haven't charted a U.S. single since "I Bet You Look Good on the Dancefloor" in 2005. Scotland's Franz Ferdinand has done better, with two hit albums and several U.S. alternative hits, including "No You Girls" in 2009, but their biggest mainstream single was "Take Me Out," which peaked at Number 66 in 2003. Folk rocker David Gray has had a smattering of U.S. album success, with the Top 60 reissue of "Babylon" (2000) being his biggest hit. The only new British act to have achieved fame in the U.S. on a Beatlesque scale is London's Coldplay, which broke through in 2000 with "Yellow," following it up with hits like "Speed of Sound" and "Viva La Vida."

Once again, as it was before the Beatles arrived, the American music scene is dominated by teen idols and heavily R&B and dance-oriented singles. Once again, pure rock bands are an endangered species on radio and TV in the era of Pro Tools; so much so that when the Strokes arrived in 2000 ("Last Nite") they were hailed as the saviors of a dying genre, much as Arcade Fire ("The Suburbs") assumed the mantle in 2010. In the meantime, bands ranging across the spectrum from heavy metal to pop rock still catch a moment or two in the ear or on the internet to keep rock fans dreaming of a better day, among them the White Stripes, Kings of Leon, Maroon 5, Linkin Park, Incubus, the Killers, Velvet Revolver, the post-punk Green Day, the ageless Foo Fighters, the spit-and-polished Nickelback, and the Air Supply-incarnate the Fray.

For those in search of Beatle footprints, they still abound, several genres wide and three generations deep, wherever the sound of psychedelic rock, sunshine pop, or baroque pop rock can be heard, whether in the form of Denver's Apples in Stereo ("Strawberryfire"), Dallas' Polyphonic Spree ("Sunshine"), Athens' of Montreal ("Every Day Feels Like Sunday"), Brooklyn's MGMT ("Love Always Remains"), or New York City's Vampire Weekend ("A-Punk").

For those in search of the real thing, 2010 brought about a historic merger of the two most famous corporations bearing the Apple name, when the Beatles finally allowed their catalog to be downloaded by visitors to the legendary song dispensary site on the internet.

If you like the Beatles, you probably already have most of these songs permanently downloaded into your brain. But now you can mix them with an earful of alternatives. And as far as alternatives, there are enough for Strawberry Fields to last forever.

SUGGESTED LISTENING

100 COVERS

While few artists can claim anywhere near 100 covers of their material, the Beatles have well into the thousands of their approximately 200 original songs. Of these covers, I have selected 100 that seem a particularly apt match of performer and song.

Peter Sellers	*Can't Buy Me Love*
Peggy Lee	*A Hard Day's Night*
Alma Cogan	*Eight Days a Week*
Ella Fitzgerald	*Savoy Truffle*
Frank Sinatra	*Something*
Nancy Sinatra	*Run for Your Life*
Mae West	*Day Tripper*
Cliff Richard	*Things We Said Today*
Joe Brown	*Here Comes the Sun*
Sandie Shaw	*Love Me Do*
The Swinging Bluejeans	*She Loves You*
The Tremeloes	*Good Day Sunshine*
The Crickets	*I Want to Hold Your Hand*
Sonny Curtis	*P.S. I Love You*
Elvis Presley	*Hey Jude*
The Miracles	*And I Love Her*
Fats Domino	*Lady Madonna*
John Mayall	*No Reply*

The Who	*I Saw Her Standing There*
Deep Purple	*We Can Work It Out*
Ozzy Osbourne	*In My Life*
War	*A Day in the Life*
Joe Cocker	*She Came in Through the Bathroom Window*
Bob Dylan	*Nowhere Man*
Joan Baez	*Eleanor Rigby*
Richie Havens	*Rocky Raccoon*
The Beach Boys	*You've Got to Hide Your Love Away*
Underground Sunshine	*Birthday*
Free Design	*Michelle*
Art Garfunkel	*I Will*
The Amboy Dukes	*I Feel Fine*
The Grateful Dead	*Lucy in the Sky with Diamonds*
Jimi Hendrix and Jim Morrison	*Tomorrow Never Knows*
MC5	*Come Together*
Aretha Franklin	*Let It Be*
Otis Redding	*Drive My Car*
The Hollies	*If I Needed Someone*
The Bee Gees	*Please Please Me*
Marianne Faithfull	*I'm a Loser*
James Taylor	*Yesterday*
Billy Preston	*Blackbird*
Todd Rundgren	*While My Guitar Gently Weeps*
David Bowie	*This Boy*
Tiny Tim	*Girl*
Jeff Beck	*She's a Woman*
Harry Nilsson	*You Can't Do That*
The Carpenters	*Ticket to Ride*
10cc	*Paperback Writer*
John Denver	*Mother Nature's Son*
Elton John	*Get Back*
Billy Joel	*I'll Cry Instead*

Nils Lofgren	*Any Time at All*
Blood, Sweat & Tears	*Got to Get You into My Life*
Cheap Trick	*Magical Mystery Tour*
Jeff Lynne	*With a Little Help from My Friends / Nowhere Man*
Supertramp	*Two of Us*
Elvis Costello	*All You Need Is Love*
The Damned	*Help!*
Dead Kennedys	*Back in the USSR*
Billy Bragg	*Revolution*
Paul Weller	*Don't Let Me Down*
Siouxsie & the Banshees	*Dear Prudence*
Lydia Lunch	*Why Don't We Do It in the Road*
Patti Smith	*Within You Without You*
Rosanne Cash	*I Don't Want to Spoil the Party*
Emmylou Harris	*Here, There and Everywhere*
The Dillards	*I've Just Seen a Face*
Steve Earle	*I'm Looking Through You*
Rickie Lee Jones	*For No One*
Bryan Ferry	*You Won't See Me*
Robin Gibb	*Oh! Darling*
XTC	*Strawberry Fields Forever*
Flamin' Groovies	*Misery*
The Residents	*Revolution 9*
The Feelies	*Everybody's Got Something to Hide (Except Me and My Monkey)*
Tanya Donelly	*Long Long Long*
The Pixies	*Wild Honey Pie*
Husker Du	*Helter Skelter*
Matthew Sweet and Susanna Hoffs	*And Your Bird Can Sing*
U2	*Rain*
Suede	*Across the Universe*

Stevie Ray Vaughan	*Taxman*
Bjork	*Fool on the Hill*
Oasis	*I Am the Walrus*
World Party	*Happiness Is a Warm Gun*
Cornershop	*Norwegian Wood*
The Corrs	*The Long and Winding Road*
Tori Amos	*She's Leaving Home*
Smash Mouth	*Getting Better*
Amy Winehouse	*All My Loving*
Michelle Shocked	*Lovely Rita*
They Might Be Giants	*Yellow Submarine*
Rancid	*Ob-La-Di, Ob-La-Da*
She and Him	*I Should Have Known Better*
Elliott Smith	*Because*
Sufjan Stevens	*What Goes On*
Maroon 5	*If I Fell*
Jonas Brothers	*Hello Goodbye*
Julian Lennon	*When I'm 64*
Sean Lennon	*Julia*

EARLY COVERS

In their early days, Lennon and McCartney parceled out a few of their slightly substandard songs to other local acts, who usually did quite well with them. Chart numbers are for the UK.

Love of the Loved	Cilla Black	1963 #35
I Wanna Be Your Man	The Rolling Stones	1963 #12 B side U.S.
I'm in Love	The Foremost	1963 #9
Hello Little Girl	The Foremost	1963 #17
Tip of My tongue	Tommy Quickly	1963—
I'll Be on My Way	Billy J. Kramer and the Dakotas	1963 B side
Do You Want to Know a Secret	Billy J. Kramer and the Dakotas	1963 #1 B side U.S.

Bad to Me	Billy J. Kramer and the Dakotas	1963 #1 #9 U.S.
I'll Keep You Satisfied	Billy J. Kramer and the Dakotas	1963 #5 #30 U.S.
From a Window	Billy J. Kramer and the Dakotas	1964 #10 #23 U.S.
It's for You	Cilla Black	1964 #7 #79 U.S.
A World Without Love	Peter and Gordon	1964 #1 #1 U.S.
Like Dreamers Do	Applejacks	1964 #20
Nobody I Know	Peter and Gordon	1964 #10 #12 U.S.
I Don't Want to See You Again	Peter and Gordon	1964—#16 U.S.
One and One Is Two	The Strangers with Mike Shannon	1964—
That Means a Lot	P. J. Proby	1965 #30
If You've Got Trouble	The Bristols	1965—
You've Got to Hide Your Love Away	The Silkie	1965 #28#10 U.S.
Woman	Peter and Gordon	1966 #28 #14 U.S.
Step Inside Love	Cilla Black	1967 #8
Cat Call (Catswalk)	Chris Barber	1967—
Goodbye	Mary Hopkin	1969 #2 #13 U.S.
It's Four You	The Beatnix	(Raven, 1998)

An import album containing most of these tracks, as sung by a Swedish Beatle tribute band

CHAPTER BY CHAPTER

Pre-Beatles

The Beach Boys	*Surfin' Safari* (Capitol, 1962) *Surfin' U.S.A.* (Capitol, 1963) *Surfer Girl* (Capitol, 1963) *Little Deuce Coupe* (Capitol, 1963)
The Four Seasons	*Sherry and 11 Others* (Vee Jay, 1962 *Big Girls Don't Cry and Twelve Others* (Vee Jay, 1963)

The Four Seasons *(continued)*	*Ain't That a Shame and 11 Others* (Vee Jay, 1963)
	Golden Hits of the 4 Seasons (Vee Jay, 1963)
The Kingsmen	*The Kingsmen in Person* (Wand, 1964)
Dick Dale and His Del-tones	*Surfer's Choice* (Deltone, 1963)
	Checkered Flag (Capitol, 1963)
The Surfaris	*Wipe Out* (Dot, 1963)
	The Surfaris Play Wipe Out and Others (Dot, 1963)
Trashmen	*Surfin' Bird* (Garrett, 1964)

Crossing Over

Cliff Richard	*It's All in the Game* (Epic, 1964)
The Shadows	*The Shadows* (EMI, 1961)
	Out of the Shadows (EMI, 1962)
Joe Meek	*The Legendary Joe Meek* (Castle Pulse, 2005)
Tornadoes	*The Original Telstar* (London, 1963)
Screaming Lord Sutch	*Lord Sutch and Heavy Friends* (Wounded Bird, 1970)
	Hands of Jack the Ripper (Wounded Bird, 1972)
Lonnie Donegan	*More Tops with Lonnie* (Pye, 1961)
	Golden Age of Lonnie Donegan (Golden Guinea, 1962)
Frank Ifield	*Jolly What! The Beatles and Frank Ifield* (Vee Jay, 1964)
Joe Brown and the Bruvvers	*The Piccadilly/Pye Anthology* (Piccadilly, 1994)
Tommy Steele	*Half a Sixpence* (RCA Victor, 1965)
Billy Fury	*The Sound of Fury* (Decca, 1960)
Vince Taylor and the Playboys	*Le Rock C'est Ca!* (Universal, 2003)
Tony Sheridan	*The Beatles with Tony Sheridan and Guests* (MGM, 1964)
Johnny Kidd and the Pirates	*I'll Never Get Over You* (HMV, 1963)
	The Best of Johnny Kidd and the Pirates (EMI, 2008)

Helen Shapiro	*Helen in Nashville* (See For Miles, 1963)
Cilla Black	*Is It Love?* (Capitol, 1965)
	Cilla (Parlophone, 1965)
	Cilla Sings a Rainbow (Parlophone, 1966)

The Great American Songbook

Meredith Willson	*The Music Man (Original Cast)* (Capitol, 1958)
	The Music Man (Soundtrack) (Warner Bros., 1962)
Peggy Lee	*Latin á La Lee* (Capitol, 1960)
Dinah Washington	*September in the Rain* (Mercury, 1963)
Doris Day	*On Moonlight Bay* (Columbia, 1951)
Frank Sinatra	*This Is Sinatra* (Capitol, 1956)
Fats Waller	*The Very Best of Fats Waller* (Collector's Choice, 2000)
Les Paul	*The Hit Makers* (Capitol, 1953)
Mae West	*Way Out West* (Tower, 1966)
The Ink Spots	*The Anthology* (MCA, 1998)

Rockabilly

Johnny Burnette and the Rock 'n Roll Trio	*Johnny Burnette and the Rock 'n Roll Trio* (Coral, 1956)
Eddie Cochran	*Eddie Cochran* (Liberty, 1960)
	Cherished Memories (Liberty, 1962)
	Memorial Album (Liberty, 1962)
	Singing to My Baby (Liberty, 1962)
Gene Vincent	*Bluejean Bop* (Capitol, 1956)
	Gene Vincent and His Blue Caps (Capitol, 1957)
	Gene Vincent Rocks! And the Blue Caps Roll (Capitol, 1958)
Roy Orbison	*Crying* (Monument, 1962)
	Roy Orbison's Greatest Hits (Monument, 1962)
	In Dreams (Monument, 1963)
Carl Perkins	*Dance Album of Carl Perkins* (Sun, 1958)
	Whole Lotta Shakin' (Columbia, 1958)

Eddie Fontaine	*Rock with Me* (Charly, 1988)
Chan Romero	*Hippy Hippy Shake* (Del-Fi, 1995)
The Everly Brothers	*The Everly Brothers* (Cadence, 1958)
	It's Everly Time (Warner Bros., 1960)
	The Fabulous Style of the Everly Brothers (Warner Bros., 1960)
	A Date with the Everly Brothers (Warner Bros., 1960)
	The Golden Hits of the Everly Brothers (Warner Bros., 1960)
Elvis Presley	*Elvis Presley* (RCA Victor, 1956)
	Elvis (RCA Victor, 1956)
	Love Me Tender (RCA Victor, 1956)
	Lovin' You (RCA Victor, 1957)
	Jailhouse Rock (RCA Victor, 1957)
	King Creole (RCA Victor, 1958)
	For LP Fans Only (RCA Victor, 1959)
	A Date with Elvis (RCA Victor, 1959)
	Elvis Is Back (RCA Victor, 1960)
	G. I. Blues (RCA Victor, 1960)
	Flaming Star (RCA Victor, 1960)
	Something for Everybody (RCA Victor, 1961)
	Wild in the Country (RCA Victor, 1961)
	Blue Hawaii (RCA Victor, 1961)
	Pot Luck (RCA Victor, 1962)
	Follow That Dream (RCA Victor, 1962)
	Kid Galahad (RCA Victor, 1962)
	Girls! Girls! Girls! (RCA Victor, 1962)
	It Happened at the World's Fair (RCA Victor, 1962)
	Fun in Acapulco (RCA Victor, 1963)
Wanda Jackson	*Rockin' with Wanda* (Capitol, 1960)

Rhythm & Blues

Little Richard	*Here's Little Richard* (Specialty, 1957)
Larry Williams	*Here's Larry Williams* (Specialty, 1959)
Fats Domino	*Fats Is Back* (Reprise, 1968)
The Shirelles	*Greatest Hits* (Scepter, 1963)
The Chiffons	*Sweet Talkin' Guy* (Laurie, 1960)
Little Willie John	*Fever* (King, 1956)
Little Eva	*Llllloco-Motion* (Dimension, 1962)

Ray Charles	*Ray Charles* (Atlantic, 1958) *The Great Ray Charles* (Atlantic, 1959) *What'd I Say* (Atlantic, 1959) *The Genius of Ray Charles* (Atlantic, 1962)
Piano Red	*The American Roots of the British Invasion* (Varese Sarabande, 2002)
Roy Lee Johnson	*Roy Lee Johnson and the Villagers* (Stax, 1973)
Joey Dee & the Starliters	*Doin' the Twist, Recorded Live at the* *Peppermint Lounge* (Roulette, 1961) *Hey, Let's Twist!* (Roulette, 1962) *Back at the Peppermint Lounge / Twistin' with* *Joey Dee and His Starliters* (Roulette, 1962)
The Isley Brothers	*Twist and Shout* (Wand, 1962)
The Miracles	*The Fabulous Miracles* (Tamla, 1963) *The Miracles on Stage* (Tamla, 63) *Doin' Mickey's Monkey* (Tamla, 1963)
Mary Wells	*Two Lovers and Other Great Hits* (Motown, 1963) *Love Songs to the Beatles* (20th Century Fox, 1965)
The Marvelettes	*Greatest Hits* (Tamla, 1966)
James Ray	*James Ray* (Caprice, 1961)
Arthur Alexander	*You Better Move On* (Dot, 1962)

The Songwriters

Chuck Berry	*After School Session* (Chess, 1958) *One Dozen Berrys* (Chess, 1959) *Berry on Top* (Chess, 1960) *Chuck Berry on Stage* (Chess, 1963) *Newest Juke Box Hits* (Chess, 1964) *St. Louis to Liverpool* (Chess, 1964)
The Crickets	*The Chirping Crickets* (Coral, 1958)
Buddy Holly	*The Complete Buddy Holly* (MCA, 1969)
Jackie De Shannon	*Jackie De Shannon* (Collector's Choice, 1963) *Don't Turn Your Back on Me* (Liberty, 1964)
Jerry Leiber and Mike Stoller	*The Leiber and Stoller Story, Vols. 1, 2, 3* (Ace, 2004-07)

Phil Spector	*Greatest Hits* (Warner Bros., 1977) *Back to Mono* (ABKCO, 1991)
The Ronettes	*Presenting the Fabulous Ronettes Featuring Veronica* (Philles, 1964)
Ronnie Spector	*Siren* (Polish, 1980) *Unfinished Business* (Columbia, 1987)
The Coasters	*The Coasters* (Atco, 1956) *Greatest Hits* (Atco, 1958) *One by One* (Atco, 1960) *Coast Along* (Atco, 1961)

Doc Pomus and
  Mort Shuman
Gerry Goffin and
  Carole King
Barry Mann and
  Cynthia Weil
	The Brill Building Sound (Era, 93)

Carole King	*Pearls: Songs of Goffin and King* (Scarface, 1980)
Burt Bacharach and Hal David	*Reach Out* (A&M, 1967) *Make It Easy on Yourself* (A&M, 1969)
Jeff Barry and Ellie Greenwich	*Let It Be Written, Let It Be Sung* (Verve, 1973)

George Martin

Monty Python	*Matching Tie and Handkerchief* (Arista, 1973)
The Firesign Theater	*Don't Crush That Dwarf, Hand Me the Pliers* (Columbia, 1970)
Flanders and Swann	*At the Drop of a Hat* (EMI, 1960) *At the Drop of Another Hat* (EMI, 1964)
Johnny Dankworth	*The Best of Johnny Dankworth* (Redial, 1999)
Cleo Laine	*Born on a Friday* (RCA Victor, 1976)
Jimmy Shand	*Bluebell Polka* (Castle, 2007)
Rolf Harris	*Tie Me Kangaroo Down, Sport & Sun Arise* (Epic, 1963)
The Vipers	*The Coffee Bar Session* (Parlophone, 1957)
Matt Monro	*My Kind of Girl* (Warwick, 1961)
The Action	*Rolled Gold* (Reaction, 2002)

David and Jonathan	*Michelle* (Capitol, 1966)
Ivor Cutler	*Who Tore Your Trousers* (Decca, 1961)
	Ludo (Rev-Ola, 1967)
The Scaffold	*Lily the Pink* (Parlophone, 1969)
Edwards Hand	*Edwards Hand* (Lightning Tree Eire, 1969)
	Stranded (Lightning Tree Eire, 1970)
	Rainshine (Regal Zonophone, 1971)
Mahavishnu Orchestra	*Apocalypse* (Columbia, 1974)
America	*Holiday* (Warner Bros., 1974)
	Hearts (Warner Bros., 1975)
	Hideaway (Warner Bros.,1976)
	Harbor (Warner Bros., 1977)
Jeff Beck	*Blow by Blow* (Epic, 1976)
	Wired (Epic, 1977)
American Flyer	*American Flyer* (United Artists, 1976)
Jimmy Webb	*El Mirage* (Collector's Choice, 1977)
Neil Sedaka	*A Song* (Elektra, 1977)
Paul McCartney	*Tug of War* (Columbia, 1982)
Various	*Produced by George Martin* (Capitol, 2001)

Folk Rock

The Animals	*The Animals* (MGM, 1964)
Bob Dylan	*Another Side of Bob Dylan* (Columbia, 1965)
	Highway 61 Revisited (Columbia, 1965)
	Blonde on Blonde (Columbia, 1966)
The Brothers Four	*A Beatles Songbook* (Columbia, 1966)
The Byrds	*Mr. Tambourine Man* (Columbia, 1965)
	Turn! Turn! Turn! (Columbia, 1966)
	Fifth Dimension (Columbia, 1966)
Simon and Garfunkel	*Wednesday Morning, 3 AM* (Columbia, 1966)
	Sounds of Silence (Columbia, 1966)
The Association	*And Then . . . Along Comes the Association* (Warner Bros., 1966)
Donovan	*Sunshine Superman* (Epic, 1966)
The Lovin' Spoonful	*Daydream* (Kama Sutra, 1966)
	Hums of the Lovin' Spoonful (Kama Sutra, 1966)

Acid Rock

The Beach Boys	*Pet Sounds* (Capitol, 1966)
The Steve Miller Band	*Your Saving Grace* (Capitol, 1969)
Frank Zappa and the Mothers of Invention	*Freak Out* (Verve, 1967)
	We're Only in It for the Money (Verve, 1968)
Ravi Shankar	*Live at Monterey* (EMI/Angel, 1998)
The Incredible String Band	*The 5000 Spirits or Layers of the Onion* (Elektra, 1967)
Pink Floyd	*The Piper at the Gates of Dawn* (EMI, 1967)
The Bonzo Dog Doo-Dah Band	*Gorilla* (Liberty, 1967)
Tomorrow	*Tomorrow* (EMI, 1968)
Traffic	*Mr. Fantasy* (Island, 1967)

The American Beatles

The Remains	*The Remains* (*Epic,* 66)
The Monkees	*The Monkees* (Colgems, 1966)
	More of the Monkees (Colgems, 1967)
	Headquarters (Colgems, 1967)
	Pisces, Aquarius, Capricorn & Jones Ltd (Colgems, 1967)
The Left Banke	*Walk Away Renee / Pretty Ballerina* (Smash, 1967)
Love	*Forever Changes* (Elektra, 1967)
The Merry-Go-Round	*The Merry-Go-Round* (A&M, 1967)
Harry Nilsson	*Pandemonium Shadow Show* (RCA, 1968)
Montage	*Montage* (Laurie, 1969)
Stories	*Stories* (Kama Sutra, 1972)
The Beckies	*The Beckies* (Sire, 1976)
The Grass Roots	*Let's Live for Today* (Dunhill, 1967)
The Beau Brummels	*Introducing the Beau Brummels* (Autumn, 1965)
13th Floor Elevators	*The Psychedelic Sounds of the 13th Floor Elevators* (Sunspots, 66)
Emitt Rhodes	*Emitt Rhodes* (Dunhill, 1970)

Todd Rundgren	*Something / Anything* (Bearsville, 1972)
Raspberries	*Raspberries* (Capitol, 1972)
	Fresh (Capitol, 1973)
	Side Three (Capitol, 1973)
	Starting Over (Capitol, 1974)
Eric Carmen	*Eric Carmen* (Arista, 1975)
Big Star	*#1 Record* (Ardent, 1972)
Alex Chilton	*Like Flies on Sherbert* (Peabody, 1979)
Cheap Trick	*In Color* (Epic, 1977)
The Knack	*Get the Knack* (Capitol, 1979)
	But the Little Girls Understand (Capitol, 1980)
The Romantics	*Romantics* (Nemperor, 1980)
Tommy Tutone	*Tommy Tutone 2* (Columbia, 1981)
Utopia	*Deface the Music* (Bearsville, 1980)
Beatlemania	*Original Cast Recording* (Pair, 1977)
Various	*Sgt. Pepper's Lonely Hearts Club Band (Soundtrack)* (RSO, 1978)

Apple Records

James Taylor	*James Taylor* (Apple, 1969)
Mary Hopkin	*Postcard* (Apple, 1969)
Jackie Lomax	*Is This What You Want?* (Apple, 69)
Badfinger	*Magic Christian Music* (Apple, 1970)
	No Dice (Apple, 1970)
	Straight Up (Apple, 1971)
Billy Preston	*That's the Way God Planned It* (Apple, 69)
Yoko Ono	*Yoko Ono / Plastic Ono Band* (Apple, 1971)
	Fly (Apple, 1971)
	Approximately Infinite Universe (Apple, 1973)
	Feeling the Space (Apple, 1973)
Elephant's Memory	*Elephant's Memory* (Apple, 72)
David Peel	*The Pope Smokes Dope* (Apple, 73)

The Anti-Beatles

Led Zeppelin	*Led Zeppelin* (Atlantic, 1969)
The Velvet Underground	*The Velvet Underground and Nico* (Verve, 1967)

The Stooges	*The Stooges* (Elektra, 1969)
John Lennon	*John Lennon / Plastic Ono Band* (Apple, 1970)
Harry Nilsson	*Pussy Cats* (RCA, 1974)
David Bowie	*The Rise and Fall of Ziggy Stardust and the Spiders from Mars* (RCA, 1972)
New York Dolls	*New York Dolls* (Mercury, 1973)
Lou Reed	*Transformer* (RCA, 1972)
Gary Glitter	*Glitter* (Bell, 1972)
Ramones	*Ramones* (Sire, 1976)
The Rutles	*The Rutles* (Warner Bros., 1978)
Devo	*Q: Are We Not Men? A: We Are Devo!* (Warner Bros., 1978)
X-Ray Spex	*Germ Free Adolescents* (Virgin, 1978)
Siouxsie and the Banshees	*The Scream* (Polydor, 1978)
Lydia Lunch	*Stateless* (Stiff, 1979)
Elvis Costello	*Spike* (Warner Bros., 1989)

The American Roots Revival

Elvis Presley	*From Elvis in Memphis* (RCA, 1969)
Tom Petty and the Heartbreakers	*Tom Petty and the Heartbreakers* (Shelter, 1977)
Shoes	*Present Tense* (Elektra, 1979) *Tongue Twister* (Elektra, 1981)
Robert Gordon	*Robert Gordon with Link Wray* (Private Stock, 1977) *Fresh Fish Special* (Private Stock, 1978)
Marshall Crenshaw	*Marshall Crenshaw* (Warner Bros., 1982)
Flamin' Groovies	*Shake Some Action* (Sire, 1976)
Dave Edmunds	*Repeat When Necessary* (Swan Song, 1979)
Rockpile	*Seconds of Pleasure* (Columbia, 1980)
The Everly Brothers	*EV84* (Mercury, 1984) *Born Yesterday* (Mercury, 1986)
Stray Cats	*Built for Speed* (EMI-America, 1982)
R.E.M.	*Murmur* (I.R.S., 1983) *Reckoning* (I.R.S., 1984)
Guided by Voices	*Bee Thousand* (Scat, 1994)

Jonathan Richman	*Modern Lovers* (Beserkley, 1976) *Jonathan Richman & the Modern Lovers* (Beserkley, 1977) *Rock & Roll with the Modern Lovers* (Beserkley, 1977)
The Smithereens	*Meet the Smithereens* (Koch, 2007) *B-Sides the Beatles* (Koch, 2009)
The Feelies	*Only Life* (A&M, 1988)
Fountains of Wayne	*Welcome Interstate Managers* (S-Curve, 2003)
They Might Be Giants	*Lincoln* (Bar/None, 1988)
Barenaked Ladies	*Gordon* (Reprise, 1992)
Ween	*The Mollusk* (Elektra, 1997)
Goo Goo Dolls	*A Boy Named Goo* (Warner Bros., 1995)
10,000 Maniacs	*In My Tribe* (Elektra, 1987)
The Replacements	*Let It Be* (Twin Tone, 1984)
The Three O'Clock	*Arrive Without Traveling* (I.R.S., 1985)
Bangles	*All Over the Place* (Columbia, 1984)
The Lemonheads	*It's a Shame About Ray* (Atlantic, 1992)
'Til Tuesday	*Voices Carry* (Epic, 1985)
Steve Earle	*Guitar Town* (MCA, 1986)
R. Stevie Moore	*Meet the R. Stevie Moore* (Cherry Red, 2008)
Indigo Girls	*Indigo Girls* (Epic, 1989)
Jellyfish	*Bellybutton* (Charisma, 1990)
Neutral Milk Hotel	*In the Aeroplane Over the Sea* (British Domino, 1998)
Gin Blossoms	*New Miserable Experience* (A&M, 1993)
Weezer	*Weezer* (DGC, 1994)
The Wallflowers	*Bringing Down the Horse* (Interscope, 1996)
Belly	*Star* (Sire, 1993)
Traveling Wilburys	*Volume One* (Wilbury, 1988) *Volume Three* (Wilbury, 1990)
Fraternal Order of the All	*Greetings from Planet Love* (Dome, 1998)
Modest Mouse	*This Is a Long Drive for Someone with Nothing to Think About* (Up, 1996)
The Shins	*Oh, Inverted World* (Sub Pop, 2001) *Chutes Too Narrow* (Sub Pop, 2003) *Wincing the Night Away* (Sub Pop, 2007)

| The Postal Service | *Give Up* (Sub Pop, 2004) |

The British Invasions

Beaver and Krause	*In a Wild Sanctuary* (Warner Bros., 1970)
Walter Carlos	*Switched-On Bach* (Columbia, 1969)
Dick Hyman	*Moog: The Electric Eclectics of Dick Hyman* (Command, 1969)
Gershon Kingsley	*Music to Moog By* (Dagored, 1969)
Hot Butter	*Popcorn* (Musicor, 1972)
Gary Numan	*The Pleasure Principle* (Beggar's Banquet, 1979)
Gerry and the Pacemakers	*Don't Let the Sun Catch You Crying* (Laurie, 1964)
	Gerry and the Pacemakers' Second Album (Laurie, 1964)
	Ferry Cross the Mersey (United Artists, 1965)
The Dave Clark Five	*Glad All Over* (Epic, 1964)
	The Dave Clark Five Return (Epic, 1964)
	American Tour (Epic, 1964)
	Coast to Coast (Epic, 1965)
	Weekend in London (Epic, 1965)
	Having a Wild Weekend (Epic, 1965)
	I Like It Like That (Epic, 1965)
Herman's Hermits	*Introducing Herman's Hermits* (MGM, 1965)
	Herman's Hermits On Tour (MGM, 1965)
	The Best of Herman's Hermits (MGM, 1965)
The Seekers	*The Seekers* (Marvel, 1965)
	The New Seekers (Capitol, 1965)
	A World of Our Own (Capitol, 1965)
The Kinks	*You Really Got Me* (Reprise, 1964)
	Kinks-Size (Reprise, 1965)
	Kinda Kinks (Reprise, 1965)
	Kinks Kinkdom (Reprise, 1965)
	The Kink Kontroversy (Reprise, 1966)
	Kinks Greatest Hits (Reprise, 1966)
	Face to Face (Reprise, 1967)
	The Live Kinks (Reprise, 1967)
	Something Else by the Kinks (Reprise, 1968)
	Arthur (Or the Decline and Fall of the British Empire) (Reprise, 1969)
The Rolling Stones	*England's Newest Hitmakers* (London, 1964)

	12 x 5 (London, 1964)
	The Rolling Stones, Now! (London, 1965)
	Out of Our Heads (London, 1965)
	December's Children (and Everybody's) (London, 1965)
	Big Hits (High Tide and Green Grass) (London, 1966)
	After-Math (London, 1966)
	Got Live if You Want It (London, 1966)
	Between the Buttons (London, 1967)
	Flowers (London, 1967)
	Their Satanic Majesties Request (London, 1967)
	Beggars Banquet (London, 1968)
	Through the Past, Darkly (Big Hits, Vol. 2) (London, 1969)
	Let It Bleed (London, 1969)
Billy J. Kramer and the Dakotas	*Little Children* (Imperial, 1965)
The Yardbirds	*For Your Love* (Epic, 1965)
	Having a Rave Up (Epic, 1965)
	Over Under Sideways Down (Epic, 1966)
	Yardbirds' Greatest Hits (Epic, 1967)
	Little Games (Epic, 1967)
The Hollies	*Hear! Here!* (Imperial, 1966)
	Bus Stop (Imperial, 1966)
	Stop! Stop! Stop! (Imperial, 1967)
	The Hollies' Greatest Hits (Imperial, 1967)
	Evolution (Epic, 1967)
The Who	*The Who Sell Out* (Decca, 1968)
The Jeff Beck Group	*Truth* (Sony Music Distributor, 1968)
	Beck-ola (Sony Music Distributor, 1969)
The Zombies	*Odyssey and Oracle* (Date, 1969)
The Troggs	*Wild Thing* (Fontana, 196)
Roy Head	*Treat Me Right* (Scepter, 1965)
Georgie Fame	*Yeh Yeh* (Imperial, 1965)
Traffic	*Traffic* (Unitied Artists, 1968)
The Bee Gees	*Bee Gees' First* (Atco, 1967)
	Horizontal (Atco, 1968)
	Idea (Atco, 1968)
	Odessa (Atco, 1969)

The Small Faces	*There Are but Four Small Faces* (Immediate, 1966)
Rod Stewart	*The Rod Stewart Album* (Mercury, 1969) *Gasoline Alley* (Mercury, 1969)
Electric Light Orchestra	*Eldorado* (United Artists, 1974)
10cc	*Sheet Music* (UK, 1974) *The Original Soundtrack* (Mercury, 1975) *100 cc* (UK, 1975)
Liverpool Echo	*Liverpool Echo* (Rev-Ola, 2005)
Bay City Rollers	*Bay City Rollers* (Arista, 1975) *Rock n' Roll Love Letter* (Arista, 1976) *Dedication* (Arista, 1976) *It's a Game* (Arista, 1977)
Supertramp	*Crime of the Century* (A&M, 1974) *Crisis? What Crisis?* (A&M, 1975) *Even in the Quietest Moments* (A&M, 1977) *Breakfast in America* (A&M, 1978)
Squeeze	*Argybargy* (A&M, 1980) *East Side Story* (A&M, 1981) *Sweets from a Stranger* (A&M, 1982) *Singles: 45's and Under* (A&M, 1983)
XTC	*Skylarking* (Geffen, 1986)
Bananarama	*Deep Sea Skiving* (London, 1983) *Bananarama* (London, 1984) *True Confessions* (London, 1986) *Wow!* (London, 1987)
Prefab Sprout	*Two Wheels Good* (Epic, 1985)
Crowded House	*Crowded House* (Capitol, 1986) *Temple of Low Men* (Capitol, 1988)
World Party	*Private Revolution* (Chrysalis, 1986) *Goodbye Jumbo* (Chrysalis, 1991 *Thank You World* (Chrysalis, 1993)
The La's	*The La's* (Go! Discs, 1990)
Boo Radleys	*Ichabod and I* (Action, 1990)
Stone Roses	*Stone Roses* (Silvertone, 1990)
Suede	*Suede* (Nude/Columbia, 1993)
Belle and Sebastian	*Tigermilk* (Jeepster, 1999)
Cornershop	*When I Was Born for the 7th Time* (Luaka Bop, 1998)

Oasis	*(What's the Story) Morning Glory* (Creation, 1995)
Spice Girls	*Spice* (Virgin, 1997) *Spiceworld* (Virgin, 1997)
New Kids on the Block	*Hangin' Tough* (Columbia, 1988)
Hanson	*Middle of Nowhere* (Mercury, 1997)
Backstreet Boys	*Backstreet Boys* (Jive, 1997)
'N Sync	*'N Sync* (RCA, 1998)
The Jonas Brothers	*It's About Time* (Columbia, 2006)

Here Today

Various	*I Am Sam (Soundtrack)* (V2, 2002)
Various	*Across the Universe (Soundtrack)* (Interscope, 2002)
Various	*Nowhere Boy (Soundtrack)* (Sony, 2010)
The Beatles / Cirque du Soleil	*Love* (*The Beatles Album*) (Apple / Capitol, 2006)
Circue du Soleil	*All Together Now* (DVD) (Apple Corp., 2006)
Paul McCartney	*Memory Almost Full* (Universal, 2007)
Bob Dylan	*Together Through Life* (Columbia, 2009)
Westlife	*Westlife* (Arista, 2000)
Robbie Williams	*The Ego Has Landed* (Capitol, 1999)
Coldplay	*Parachutes* (Netwerk, 2000) *A Rush of Blood to the Head* (Capitol, 2002)
James Blunt	*Back to Bedlam* (Custard, 2005)
David Gray	*White Ladder* (ATO, 2000)
Travis	*The Man Who* (Independente, 2000)
Franz Ferdinand	*Franz Ferdinand* (Domino, 2004)
Arctic Monkeys	*Whatever People Say I Am, That's What I'm Not* (Domino, 2006)
Apples in Stereo	*Her Wallpaper Reverie* (SpinArt, 1999)
Strokes NYC	*Is This Is* (RCA, 2001) *Rooms on Fire* (RCA, 2004)
Polyphonic Spree	*Together We Are Heavy* (Hollywood, 2004)
Of Montreal	*The Sunlandic Twins* (Polyvinyl, 2005)
Vampire Weekend	*Vampire Weekend* (XL, 2008)
MGMT	*Time to Pretend* (EP) (Cantara, 2009)
Arcade Fire	*The Suburbs* (Merge, 2010)

The Beatles Day by Day: The Originals (Mischief, 09)
If you only want to listen to one album to understand where the
Beatles came from, this is the one to get, even if it has four sides
and eighty-one tracks. Conceived to replicate the jam session the
Beatles engaged in prior to tackling the *Let It Be* album, with all the
original artists, this is about the best cross section of American rock
and roots music around (with a ringer from England tossed in here
and there out of patriotic duty). It's also the best indication, if any
more were needed, of the Beatles' incredible knowledge of the history of music prior to their arrival in it.

As far as what happened *after* their arrival . . . I could write a
book.

DISC ONE

Shake, Rattle & Roll	Big Joe Turner
Cannonball	Duane Eddy
Short Fat Fannie	Larry Williams
Johnny B. Goode	Chuck Berry
At the Hop	Danny and the Juniors
Rip It Up	Little Richard
Take These Chains	Larry Williams
All Shook Up	Elvis Presley
Whole Lotta Shakin' Goin' On	Jerry Lee Lewis
Diggin' My Potatoes	Lonnie Donegan
Knee Deep in the Blues	Guy Mitchell
Mailman, Bring Me No More Blues	Buddy Holly
Crazy Feet	Fred Astaire
Blue Suede Shoes	Carl Perkins
Maybellene	Chuck Berry
Lawdy Miss Clawdy	Lloyd Price
Kansas City	Little Richard
Take This Hammer	Leadbelly
That's All Right	Elvis Presley
Move It	Cliff Richard

DISC TWO

Bye Bye Love	The Everly Brothers
Bo Diddley	Bo Diddley
Be Bop a Lula	Gene Vincent
Lucille	Little Richard
Midnight Special	Leadbelly
Sweet Little Sixteen	Chuck Berry
Hallelujah, I Love Her So	Ray Charles
Shake, Rattle and Roll	Big Joe Turner
The Peanut Vendor	Stan Kenton
When Irish Eyes Are Smiling	Bing Crosby
That'll Be the Day	Buddy Holly
Fools Like Me	Jerry Lee Lewis
It's Only Make Believe	Conway Twitty
Slippin' and Slidin'	Little Richard
Queen of the Hop	Bobby Darin
(You're So Square) Baby, I Don't Care	Elvis Presley
School Day	Chuck Berry
High Noon (Do Not Forsake Me)	Tex Ritter
When the Saints Go Marching In	Louis Armstrong

DISC THREE

Singing the Blues	Guy Mitchell
You Are My Sunshine	Jimmie Davis
Tiger Rag	Original Dixieland Jazz
Band	
High School Confidential	Jerry Lee Lewis
Little Demon	Screamin' Jay Hawkins
Don't Be Cruel	Elvis Presley
Your True Love	Carl Perkins
Jenny Jenny	Little Richard
Low Down Blues	Larry Williams
Ramrod	Duane Eddy
Rock Island Line	Lonnie Donegan
Right String Baby (But the Wrong Yo Yo)	Carl Perkins

Rock and Roll Music	Chuck Berry
Not Fade Away	Buddy Holly
Catch a Falling Star	Perry Como
I Got Stung	Elvis Presley
St. Louis Blues	Louis Armstrong
Send Me Some Lovin'	Little Richard
Cocaine Blues	Reverend Gary Davis
You Can't Catch Me	Chuck Berry
Leaning on a Lamppost	George Formby

DISC FOUR

Honky Tonk, Parts 1 & 2	Bill Doggett
Lotta Lovin'	Gene Vincent
Miss Ann	Little Richard
True Love	Elvis Presley
Great Balls of Fire	Jerry Lee Lewis
Smoke Stack Lightning	Howlin' Wolf
Brown Eyed Handsome Man	Chuck Berry
Gone, Gone, Gone	Carl Perkins
My Baby Left Me	Elvis Presley
Sure to Fall	Carl Perkins
Midnight Special	Lonnie Donegan
Maybe Baby	Buddy Holly
Mack the Knife	Louis Armstrong
Long Tall Sally	Little Richard
Honey Hush	Big Joe Turner
Friendship	Judy Garland and Johnny Mercer
Milkcow Blues Boogie	Elvis Presley
Tiger Rag	Duke Ellington
Thirty Days	Chuck Berry
Tea for Two	Tommy Dorsey
Adagio for Strings	NBC Symphony Orchestra

INDEX

INDEX

INDEX